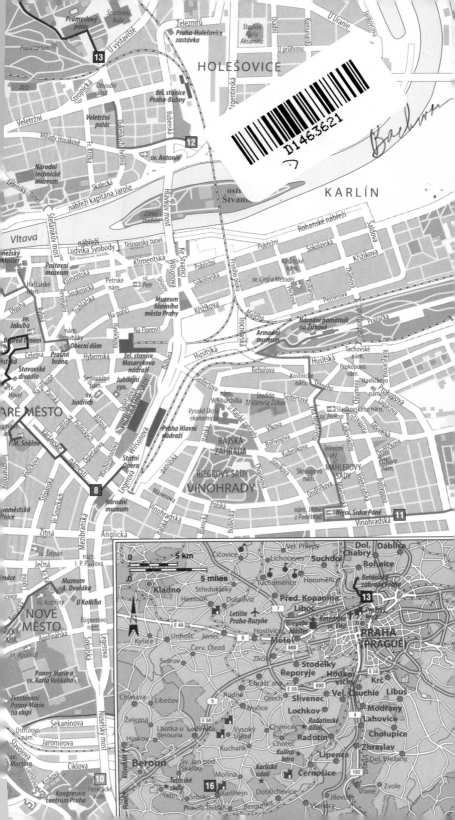

CONTENTS

ABOUT THIS BOOK

This *Step by Step Guide* has been produced by the editors of Insight Guides, whose books have set the standard for visual travel guides since 1970. With top-quality photography and authoritative recommendations, this guidebook brings you the very best of Prague in a series of 16 tailor-made tours.

WALKS AND TOURS

The tours in the book provide something to suit all budgets, tastes and trip lengths. As well as covering Prague's many classic attractions, the routes also track lesser-known sights and up-and-coming areas; there is also an excursion to Karlštejn for those who want to extend their visit outside the city centre. The tours embrace a range of interests, so whether you are an art fan, a keen hiker or have kids to entertain, you will find an option to suit.

We recommend that you read the whole of a tour before setting out. This should help you to familiarise yourself with the route and enable you to plan where to stop for refreshments –

Above: Prague highlights include the Charles Bridge, the charming streets of the Old Town, Frank Gehry's 'Fred and Ginger' Building, the Rudolfinum and the soldiers on guard at the Castle.

options for this are shown in the 'Food and Drink' boxes, recognisable by the knife-and-fork sign, on most pages.

For our pick of the walks by theme, consult Recommended Tours For… *(see pp.6–7).*

OVERVIEW

The tours are set in context by this introductory section, giving an overview of the city, plus background information on food and drink, shopping and cultural activities. A succinct history timeline highlights the key events that have shaped Prague over the centuries.

DIRECTORY

Also supporting the tours is a Directory chapter, comprising a user-friendly A–Z of practical information, our pick of where to stay while you are in the city and select restaurant listings; these eateries complement the more low-key cafés and restaurants that feature within the tours themselves and are intended to offer a wider choice for evening dining.

The Authors

Maria Lord is a writer and editor, specialising in the arts and travel (particularly Central Europe, Greece and India). She is the author of several books: recent titles include *The Story of Music,* Berlitz guides to Zakynthos and Kefallonia and Kerala, *Smart Guide Salzburg* and the forthcoming *Smart Guide Delhi.* She was the managing editor and main author for Insight's *City Guide Prague.* Michael Macaroon is a writer specialising in travel and the arts. He particularly enjoys visiting Prague for its pubs, and is worried about the recent trend for replacing them with pizzerias. Lord and Macaroon are also authors of Insight's *Smart Guide Prague.*

Margin Tips

Shopping tips, historical facts, handy hints and information on activities help visitors make the most of their time in Prague.

Feature Boxes

Notable topics are highlighted in these special boxes, which are dotted throughout the Overview and Walks and Tours chapters.

Key Facts Box

This box gives details of the distance covered on the tour, plus an estimate of how long it should take. It also states where the route starts and finishes, and gives key travel information such as which days are best to do the route, or handy transport tips.

Footers

Within the Walks and Tours chapter, look here for the tour name, a map reference and the main attraction on the double-page.

Food and Drink

Recommendations of where to stop for refreshment are given in these boxes. The numbers prior to each restaurant/café name link to references in the main text. On city maps, restaurants are plotted.

The **€** signs at the end of each entry reflect the approximate cost of a two-course meal for one, with a glass of house wine. These should be seen as a guide only. Price ranges, also quoted on the inside back flap for easy reference (and in euros for accessibility, although note that the currency in the Czech Republic is the *koruna*, or crown; Kč for short), are as follows:

€€€€	€60 and above
€€€	€40–60
€€	€20–40
€	€20 and below

Route Map

Detailed cartography shows the itinerary clearly plotted with numbered dots. For more detailed mapping, see the pull-out map slotted inside the back cover.

PARKS AND GARDENS

The city's green spaces include the gardens of the Waldstein Palace (tour 4), the University Botanical Gardens in Nové Město (tour 9) and the Prague Botanical Garden (tour 13).

RECOMMENDED TOURS FOR...

ART ENTHUSIASTS

The city's major showcases for art include the several venues at the castle (walk 1), the National Gallery (walk 2), the Strahov Collection of Art (tour 3), the Museum of the Decorative Arts (walk 7) and the Museum of Modern Art in the Functionalist Veletržní Palace (tour 12).

MUSIC LOVERS

Follow in the illustrious footsteps of Smetana (tour 5), Dvořák in Nové Město (tour 9) and Mozart in Smíchov (tour 14). Opera buffs can see the State Opera House on tour 8.

CLASSIC CAFÉS

Take time out at a traditional café in the Old Town (Staré Město), on tour 5, or check out such classic institutions as Café Slavia in Nové Město (tour 9).

CHILDREN

Kids can marvel at the albino peacocks at the Waldstein Palace on walk 4 or, on walk 13, spend time at the zoo or picnicking and playing in the park at Stromovka, once a royal hunting ground.

ARCHITECTURE BUFFS

Walk 7 is a guide to Czech architecture across the ages, while Wenceslas Square (walk 8) is a fine showcase for several of the city's architectural styles. For Modernism, visit the 'Fred and Ginger' building in Nové Město (tour 9) or the Müller Villa (tour 15). Vyšehrad (tour 10) is renowned for its Cubist designs.

HISTORY HUNTERS

First stop should be the castle (walk 1), then perhaps the Old Town (walk 5) for its historic buildings, and Josefov (walk 6), the city's Jewish Quarter. Further afield, why not visit Vyšehrad (tour 10), where, according to legend, the city was founded.

CZECH BEER

Those eager to check out the local brew should head for Smíchov (tour 14), home to the famous Staropramen Brewery, which holds hour-long historical tasting sessions.

LITERARY TYPES

Visit the Strahov Monastery's spectacular library, one of the largest in the country, on walk 3, or pay homage to the writer Franz Kafka in Josefov (tour 6).

TRAINSPOTTERS

Prague is famous for its trams, and visitors keen to know more should take tour 15, which includes the city's Transport Museum. A trip on the 'Nostalgic' Tram No. 91 might also be in order. For a ride on the Funicular Railway, follow tour 3.

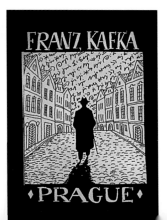

OVERVIEW

An overview of Prague's geography, customs and culture, plus illuminating background information on food and drink, shopping, culture and entertainment, and history.

INTRODUCTION

Prague is at once one of the most beautiful and intriguing cities in Europe, justly famous for its Old Town and Castle, but beyond the crowds is another equally fascinating city of galleries, gardens and iconic design.

Above from far left: St Vitus's Cathedral; papier-mâché cat in a window in the Old Town; bronze bas-relief on the Charles Bridge.

Located at the heart of Europe, Prague ('Praha' in Czech) has been the capital of the ancient realm of Bohemia for centuries. During the Middle Ages it rose to prominence as the capital of Charles IV's vast empire. As Holy Roman Emperor and ruler of much of Western Europe, he was probably the most powerful man in the world at the time (1316–78).

In the late 16th and early 17th centuries the city was the seat of the Habsburg Court and it became the capital of the newly independent country of Czechoslovakia in 1918. After a *coup d'état* in 1948, Czechs chafed under the yoke of Communist rule; but when the Iron Curtain fell in 1989, it unveiled Prague's hidden wealth of cultural treasures.

GEOGRAPHY AND LAYOUT

Prague used to be known as the 'Five Towns', and although it has now been divided into 10 separate districts, most visitors concentrate on the five historic towns: Hradčany; Staré Město (Old Town); Malá Strana (Lesser Quarter); Nové Město (New Town); and the former ghetto of the Jewish Quarter, or Josefov. The city's administration was finally unified under the rule of Joseph II (1780–90), and the separate

town halls are now mere reminders of previous autonomy.

In earlier times, the inhabitants of the congested Old Town and Jewish Quarter must have felt envious when they looked across to the New Town, where the far-sighted designs of Charles IV (1346–78) and his architects had created broad open spaces and avenues such as the Charles and Wenceslas squares. Today, however, the Old Town has been beautifully restored and the Jewish Quarter's Pařížská is a chic avenue lined with expensive shops.

The City's Growth

As the city expanded (by the beginning of the 19th century, some 80,000 people lived here), further districts were added to the original five towns. The incorporation of Vyšehrad, Holešovice and Bubeneč brought the population to around 200,000 by 1900. After World War I, the city's area tripled to a size of 550 sq km (190 sq miles), and by 1930 the population had reached 850,000.

Under Communism, new suburbs such as Severní Město (North Town) and Jižní Město (South Town) were built, and the southwestern suburb of Jihozápadní Město is a site of ongoing expansion. Today, the city has a population of around 1.2 million, while its

wider metropolitan area is estimated to accommodate over 1.9 million people.

The Vltava River

As Prague's architecture envelops you in all its glory, you could be forgiven for overlooking one of the city's most beautiful sights: the Vltava River itself, its graceful S-shape unwinding in the heart of the city. A tributary of the Elbe, and at times going under its German name of Moldau, for centuries it has inspired writers and musicians alike, notably the composer Bedřich Smetana (1824–84), whose symphonic poems dedicated to the river celebrate its lengthy journey across the Czech landscape on its way to Prague.

Architecture

Prague has one of the world's most pristine and varied cityscapes, encompassing Gothic, Renaissance, Baroque, neoclassical, Art Nouveau, Cubist and ultra-modern buildings. The centre of Prague is essentially a Gothic city with a Baroque face. Nearly all of its numerous churches were either built or remodelled during the Baroque period, and many of the original Gothic houses were given a new Baroque façade in the frenetic period of building and reconstruction initiated by the Habsburgs in the 17th century. And if the centre has a Baroque appearance, visitors who venture slightly further out might be surprised to find that Prague has some of the

Above from far left: the Charles Bridge; colourful old window; tram tracks; pretty back-street on Kampa Island.

Flooding

In August 2002, floods threatened to do more damage to Prague's historic fabric than centuries of political upheavals. Sewers overflowed and submerged streets in stinking muck. Streets buckled and buildings collapsed. Metro stations were flooded to street level. At Prague Zoo, a gorilla was drowned and an elephant and a hippo had to be shot when they could not be rescued. Fortunately, the clean-up and restoration programme went surprisingly smoothly, and today there are few remaining signs that the flooding ever took place.

Left: the neoclassical roof of the National Theatre peeks out over the riverside.

Above from far left:
tram; Petřín Hill
Observation Tower
(see p.37); cycle tour
in the Old Town;
characteristic Art
Nouveau architecture.

Above: two faces
of the elaborate
Astronomical Clock.

best examples of early 20th-century Modernist architecture of any European city.

The Communist years brought little in terms of *grands projets* to the city, but during the 1970s and 1980s, new suburbs of high-rise apartment blocks (so-called *paneláky*) were built of prefabricated concrete panels. In contrast with the experience of similar projects elsewhere in Europe, Prague's new rent-controlled estates proved quite successful, developing strong communities and attracting tenants from across the social spectrum.

Climate

As a landlocked country in Central Europe Prague tends to see continental weather patterns springing from Russia, but can experience mild, wet weather from the Atlantic. Winters are on the whole cold and wet, but it can stay dry and clear for long spells. When the wind blows from Russia, it can be extremely cold. Summers are warm but rainy. June and July are two of the rainiest months of the year, while spring and autumn are marked by changeable weather. Bring a mac or umbrella just in case.

Getting Around

Prague's public transport infrastructure is very good and consists of an integrated transport system with the metro (51 stations in total), a tram system (including the 'nostalgic tram' no. 91), buses, the Petřín funicular and three ferries. All services have a common ticketing system, and, in comparison

with public transport in many other European cities, prices are surprisingly inexpensive.

LIFE SINCE THE VELVET REVOLUTION

There have, of course, been many changes since the Velvet Revolution of 1989 for both the city and its people. Although the optimism that followed the revolution has now died down – not least as the Czechs face up to life under capitalism, membership of the European Union (EU) and Nato, and a string of corruption scandals – there is still a sense that the city is rediscovering and reinventing its past.

Sense of Identity

Some complain that city life now seems bland and somehow less vital. Feelings inherent in life in one of the smaller EU member states – a sense of powerlessness, that the action is taking place elsewhere – stand in stark contrast to the idealism and activism of intellectual life under the tyranny of Communism. Prague's days as a European centre of writers and artists have all but vanished too. Meanwhile, the younger generation has grown up with the kinds of freedoms long taken for granted by teenagers in the West, and, naturally enough, has used them to embrace consumerism.

Much, however, has been preserved. Praguers are still able to enjoy the city's intact architectural heritage, and it was fortunate to suffer considerably less damage during World War II than

many other major European cities (only a few bombing raids by the US Air Force towards the end of the war).

Prosperity

Recent years have also brought prosperity to the Czech Republic in general, and Prague in particular. The Czech economy has grown continually since 1999, and from the second quarter of 2005 to mid-2008, the rate of growth did not fall below 6 percent.

Prague itself has become the location of the European headquarters of many international companies, while its manufacturing industries – including textiles, engineering and brewing – have survived the transition to the free market. However, the city's architectural heritage has also brought a new industry that dwarfs the old: an estimated 60 percent of the city's income now derives from tourism. This in turn has allowed historic buildings to benefit from a massive renovation programme and important new buildings to be commissioned from the likes of architects Frank Gehry and Jean Nouvel. Prague is now the sixth most-visited European city after London, Paris, Rome, Madrid and Berlin, with over 3.5 million tourists each year.

On an individual level, capitalist economics have also brought relative wealth. While unemployment nationally is (at time of writing) running at approximately 5 percent (much better than the EU average), in Prague it stands at less than 2 percent, the lowest of any region in the country. Growing pressure on the labour market has led to salary growth – 5.1 percent in real terms in 2007, faster than the country's gross domestic product (4.5 percent). Moreover, the average monthly income for the capital's citizens is about 25,000Kč (roughly equivalent to £800 or $1,500 at time of writing) in comparison with about 20,000Kč for the country as a whole. Even so, the prices charged in tourist restaurants and cafés make the centre of Prague expensive for most of the capital's citizens.

Below: stained-glass Czech lion, the symbol of Bohemia.

FOOD AND DRINK

Czech food tends to the hearty and comforting end of the culinary spectrum, with a great emphasis on pork and dumplings; for those with a good appetite, it is wonderful. Even better, perhaps, is the country's delicious beer.

THE BEST GOULASH IN TOWN

Above: cow in the window of a delicatessen; ready for customers; a bold claim.

Bohemian cooking is based on the abundant produce of the country's fertile farmland, its orchards, rivers and ponds, and its vast forests teeming with game. It is unpretentious fare, intended to sustain body and soul rather than form the subject of sophisticated conversation – you are unlikely to encounter *nouvelle cuisine* – or provide a balanced range of vitamins. It can nonetheless be delicious.

WHAT TO EAT

Breakfast
The Czechs begin the day in a frugal way, with a breakfast *(snídaně)* often consisting of only a cup of coffee *(káva)* – perhaps still made in the time-honoured fashion by pouring boiling water onto finely ground beans in the cup and letting the mixture settle before attempting to drink it.

Food on the Move
Once out and about, the Praguer's appetite is likely to be whetted by the sight of one of the city's many sausage stands. Czech sausages are among the best in the world. The favourite is the *párek* (often sold in pairs as *párky*) – a Frankfurter that should really be called a Praguer as it was from here that it originated. A fatter version is called a *vuřt (cf.* German *Wurst),* while a *klobása* is an even bigger specimen – coarse-textured, with a thick skin and plenty of fatty globules. Whichever your sausage of choice, it is customary to adorn it with a dollop of mild-tasting mustard.

Marginally healthier snacks are available in the form of little open sandwiches *(obložené chlebíčky),* bought at delicatessens. Toppings may include slivers of ham, salami, hard-boiled egg, fish roe, potato salad, slices of tomato and gherkins.

Lunch
A full Czech lunch *(oběd)* will normally begin with soup *(polévka),* whether a simple meat broth *(vývar)* with dumplings, a thick potato cream soup *(bramborová)* or a bowl of tripe soup *(dršťková* – reputed to be an excellent hangover cure).

The main course is referred to half-jokingly as *vepřo-knedlo-zelo* (pork-dumpling-cabbage). Indeed, the pig is king in this country, and, fortunately for visitors, is likely to be much tastier than the sorry specimens at home. Most pigs are raised en masse, but many villagers keep a porker or two themselves. Every part is made into some tasty comestible, and the slaughter is often occasion for a

vepřové hody (pork festival). After pork, beef *(hovězí maso)* is the most popular meat, and is often served as *svíčková na smetaně,* fillet or sirloin topped with a slice of lemon and a spoonful of cranberries, and swimming in a cream sauce. Other main courses at lunchtime might include veal *(telecí maso)* or chicken *(kuře).*

The usual accompaniment to meat is the dumpling *(knedlík)* – which, in fact, enjoys even more veneration than the pig. It is made from flour, bread, potatoes or semolina, with added yeast, baking powder, eggs, milk or sugar, and is prepared in a loaf-like form and then cut with a wire (never a knife).

When it comes to vegetables, a request for anything other than cabbage will be met with raised eyebrows. Salad *(salát)* is more common, probably not in the form of tossed green lettuce, but as a medley of cucumber, onion, red pepper and tomatoes wallowing in a sweetish, vinegary sauce.

As for dessert, options are limited. There may be thin crêpes *(palačinky)* wrapped around cottage cheese *(tvaroh),* ice cream *(zmrzlina),* fruit or nuts, and perhaps served with a chocolate sauce. The dumpling makes a reappearance (like it or not), this time as an *ovocný knedlík,* filled with plums or apricots. This is really a meal in its own right, and is sometimes eaten as such, usually at home.

Cakes and Pastries

Any disappointment over dessert may easily be alleviated in Prague's cafés *(kavárna)* and patisseries *(cukrárna).*

Here, you are spoilt for choice: tarts, strudels, sponge cakes, éclairs and *koláčky* – buns filled with *tvaroh* (poppy seeds) or *povidla* (a delicious, dense, dark plum jam).

Dinner

When taken at home, the evening meal is usually a less substantial affair than lunch. But if eating out, this is the moment to move beyond *vepřo-knedlo-zelo* and sample richer dishes such as roast duck *(kachna)* or even better, roast goose *(husa).* As well as making a celebratory meal for grand occasions, geese in the Czech Republic are also forcefed to provide *husí paštíka,* liver pâté as good as the finest French *foie gras* (irresistible, as long as you don't dwell on what the unfortunate bird has had to go through).

Some restaurants will also allow you to sample the excellent variety of game reared in the fields and forests beyond Bohemia's villages. Look out for dishes featuring wild boar *(kanec),* venison *(srnčí maso),* pheasant *(bažant)* or partridge *(koroptev).*

As regards fish, Prague is a landlocked country a long way from the ocean, so it makes sense to try the freshwater kind. Roasted or fried trout *(pstruh)* features on many menus, but the quintessentially Czech fish is the carp *(kapr).* Carp are raised in their thousands in fishponds across the country. Typically netted in December, they are then brought to town, sold live from barrels and kept in the family bathtub before being slaughtered and cut into steaks, breaded and fried to

form the centrepiece of the traditional Christmas Eve dinner. In restaurants, carp is more likely to be served as *kapr na černo* in a black, sweet-and-sour sauce made mysteriously from such ingredients as nuts, raisins, sugar, beer and vinegar.

VEGETARIANS

Vegetarians will find specialist establishments catering to their needs, which is just as well since mainstream restaurants are unlikely to offer them much more than an omelette or fried cheese *(smažený sýr)*; the latter is better than it sounds, consisting of a thick slice of semi-molten local cheese (usually *hermelín*) in a breadcrumb coating and enlivened by a tasty dollop of tartare sauce.

Fungi of various descriptions may also be on offer in Prague. The environment of the Czech Republic is particularly favourable for the growth of a bewildering array of mushrooms *(houby)*, a detailed knowledge of which seems part of everyone's heritage. Fungi in all shapes and sizes are hunted down and picked in favourite spots in the countryside, brought home and fried or more likely dried, to be added later to all kinds of dishes, notably cabbage soup.

WHERE TO EAT AND DRINK

Prague restaurants *(restaurace)* vary enormously in character and price. Bargain meals are still to be had in some city-centre establishments; following office workers on their way to lunch is one way of discovering them.

Pubs and Bars

The most basic establishment is the *hostinec* or *pivnice* – beer house – a simple watering hole that also serves basic food.

Next up the ladder is the *hospoda*, the pub or beer hall. Most pubs are tied to a particular brewery, serving its product on draught in half-litre glasses. Some take great pride in the way in which they keep and serve their beer; the reputation of U zlatého Tygra (The Golden Tiger), a pub in the Old Town, is largely based on the temperature of its ancient cellars, ideal for the perfect preservation of Pilsner.

Many *hospody* serve perfectly good meals (perhaps with a more limited choice), and those at the top end of the scale may be very similar to *restaurace*.

Coffee Houses

The coffee house was one of the great institutions of the interwar First Republic. Some have faded into history – for example, the Arco, meeting place of 'Arconauts' Franz Kafka, Franz Werfel and Max Brod. Others are still in business, such as the Café Slavia *(see p.117)*, filled in its heyday with poets, painters, and actors from the National Theatre opposite.

DRINKS

The Czech Republic is home to what many consider the world's finest beers *(see right)*, but it is also wine country,

and in addition produces a number of unusual spirits and aperitifs.

Winemaking in the Czech Republic is concentrated in sunny southern Moravia, where the vines spread for almost 115km (70 miles) between the city of Brno and the Austrian and Slovak borders. Among the red wines, Frankovka (relatively dry) or Sv. Vavřinec (plummy and sweetish) can be good, while white *Ryzlink* and *Palava* go well with fish.

Bohemia's vineyards cover a much smaller area, centred on the Elbe and its tributaries north of Prague. The vines growing on the steep slope below the town of Mělník are the descendants of those brought from France and planted here by Emperor Charles IV in the 14th century. They yield white wines that are dry and rather acidic, rather like those in neighbouring Saxony.

More or less palatable fruit brandies are also distilled. The best is probably Slivovice, made from plums, though you may also try apricot brandy, *meruňkovice*, and cherry brandy, *třešňovice*. The most popular aperitif is Becherovka, a liquor originally served as a restorative to Karlsbad spa guests, and made from a secret herbal recipe. Finally, the Czech Republic is one of the few countries where absinthe is legally made and consumed.

Czech Beer

Although the oldest record of the brewer's art in Prague can be found in a document dating from 1082, the bottom-fermented Czech beers of today have evolved from the brew developed in the western Bohemian city of Plzeň (Pilsen) in 1842. The combination of local spring water, hops from Žatec in northern Bohemia, and cellaring in the ideal conditions of the sandstone caves beneath the city yielded a beer that won instant popularity – particularly in Germany, where its name, 'Pilsner' or 'Pils', is now indiscriminately applied to any pale, hoppy brew. To distinguish the original product from its imitators, its makers gave it the name of 'Pilsner Urquell' meaning 'original source' ('Plzeňský prazdroj' in Czech). Its great rival is Budčjovice – known as Budweis in German and Budvar in Czech – which comes from the southern city of České Budějovice. For those who find the distinctive sharp taste of Prazdroj a little too acidic, Budvar is a somewhat sweeter, milder drink.

Most Czech beer is of the Pilsner type, and is referred to as *svetlé* (light). It comes in two strengths, measured in degrees – indicating the amount of sugar content. What is described as '12°' *(dvánactka)* is stronger and heavier, with an alcohol content of more than 4 percent; '10°' *(desetka)* is lighter and contains less than 4 percent alcohol. As well as *svelté*, most breweries also make *tmavé*, a dark and rather sweet beer not unlike British mild. It is sometimes cut with *svelté* in an attempt to combine the advantages of both.

SHOPPING

Prague is not an international shopping destination like London, Paris or New York, but aside from the same chains you find everywhere there are some interesting local shops.

Above: puppets for sale in Josefov; quirky sign outside a commercial gallery in Staré Mešto.

Opening Times

Most shops open 10am–6pm, although those in the centre, catering largely to the tourist trade, often remain open late almost year round. On Saturdays shops outside the centre of Prague generally close at noon or 1pm; shops in the centre, especially the larger department stores, may retain weekday hours on Saturday and Sunday as well.

The centre of Prague is increasingly given over to shiny new shopping centres, which are full of international high-street chains. In addition large malls now ring the city centre. A sizeable number of international designers have set up shop along the posher avenues, although a number of Czech designers are beginning to make their mark. Service has also markedly improved since the early post-Communist days of grumpy state-employed assistants who seemed to resent your presence in their establishments.

SHOPPING AREAS

Generally the best shopping is to be found in Staré and Nové Mešto, although some of the outlying districts now have huge shopping centres. The main commercial streets of central Prague with dependably long hours all year round are Wenceslas Square (Václavské náměstí) and Na příkope. If you are looking for expensive international fashion then head for Pařížská, which runs off Old Town Square.

Some of the small streets in the Old Town, such as V Kolkovně, Dušní, Týnská and Panská, have a number of exciting and unusual boutiques. The Týn Courtyard near Old Town Square also has numerous little shops that are worth exploring, as do the back-streets of Malá Strana. If you are looking for a department store try either Kotva on náměstí Republiky or Tesco on Národní třída.

WHAT TO BUY

Czech Souvenirs

There are a number of locally produced items that are worth looking out for. You will not be able to avoid Bohemian glass and china, held in high esteem throughout the world due to their quality and fair price. New items from major manufacurers are still excellent (try Moser at Na příkope 12, or for more contemporary styles Arzenal at Valentinská 11), but now it's almost impossible to find a good deal in antiques shops. Antiques dealers have become wise to the foreign market for their wares and have altered their prices accordingly.

If you're looking for something typically Bohemian to take home as a gift, a bottle of the herbal liqueur Becherovka or some Slivovice is a good idea. Fruity wines from Bohemia and Moravia will also be appreciated. Wooden toys and puppets make excellent gift items for children. These can be found in the city-wide chain of Manufaktura shops. As well as toys

they also sell ceramics, fabrics and beautifully painted eggs.

Street vendors – concentrated in Hradčany and on the Charles Bridge – sell handmade goods, such as marionettes and costume jewellery, as well as items of dubious use and value, such as refrigerator magnets depicting famous Prague sights.

Music

Classical music CDs, especially those of Czech music from Supraphon, are cheaper than in the UK or US. The performances, by superb Czech ensembles and musicians, are always good and often thrilling. Also look out for recordings by local jazz and experimental rock musicians. Since the demise of Supraphon's own store one of the best places to find classical and contemporary music is the large Bontonland Megastore in the basement of the Koruna Building on the corner of Wenceslas Square. A good range of classical CDs can also be found at Via Musica on Malostranské náměstí.

Fashion

Although Prague seems overwhelmed by international chains and designers, local fashions by Prague designers can be found and their clothes are often interesting and well made. In Malá Strana try Pavla & Olga at Vlašská for one-offs and unusual pieces made in the shop by Pavla Michálková. In the Old Town there are a number of interesting places. Klára Nademlýnská's sexy and fashionable clothes can be had at Dlouhá 3, while Le Bohême

(Štupartská 7) has casual and classic pieces by Renáta Vokáčová. One of the most interesting places is Hard-de-Core, the brainchild of inspired designers Josefina Bakošová and Petra Krčková. This is not just a fashion shop but an institution stocking jewellery, ceramics and other handmade designs not to be found anywhere else. The owners will also design your party decorations and are happy to teach you some of their skills.

Above from far left: Bohemian glass; marionette; the elegant staircase at Kubista *(see box below)*; tourist goods in Staré Mešto.

Kubista and Modernista

These two shops are not only two of the most chic design boutiques in Prague but also also offer some of the best and most unusual souvenirs of your visit. Both capitalise on Prague's extraordinary outpouring of cutting-edge design during the first half of the 20th century. The first (Ovocný trh 19; tel: 224 236 378; www.kubista; Tue–Sun 10am–6pm), not surprisingly, concentrates on superb reproductions of Czech Cubist works, including ceramics and furniture, as well as selling a number of original pieces. Fittingly, it is located in the Cubist House of the Black Madonna. Modernista (Celetná 12; tel: 224 241 300; www. modernista.cz; Mon–Sat 11am–7pm), by contrast, concentrates on slightly later works with reproductions of pieces by Adolf Loos and Functionalist designers.

ENTERTAINMENT

Prague is famous the world over for the excellence of its classical music ensembles, from opera at the National Theatre to the Czech Philharmonic, but there is much more to explore, including jazz, theatre and film.

MUSIC

Concerts of classical music, mainly chamber ensembles, are held in many churches and historic buildings across the city. Aimed solely at tourists, the standard is not always particularly high and the repertory can be fairly predictable. However, there are some exceptional venues, putting on some of the best concerts to be heard anywhere.

The Czech Philharmonic is one of the world's great orchestras, and seeing one of its concerts at the Rudolfinum is a real event. The city's other major resident orchestra is the Prague Symphony Orchestra. Less well known than the Czech Philharmonic but still excellent, it puts on its concerts in the splendid Obecní dům *(see p.63)* from September to June. A third orchestra, the Prague Radio Symphony Orchestra, is also resident in the city. Although primarily a recording ensemble for Czech Radio, it puts on a fine concert series in the Rudolfinum between October and March. It is an outstanding orchestra, often including contemporary works in its programmes.

One of the most high-profile chamber ensembles is the Suk Chamber Orchestra, named after the violinist and composer Josef Suk (b.1929) and founded in 1974. It tends to concentrate on the core Czech repertory. Two orchestras established since 1989 and starting to make an international name for themselves are the Prague Philharmonia, which puts on an interesting mix of concerts at various locations in Prague, and the Czech National Symphony Orchestra.

Opera and Ballet

The quality of opera performances in Prague is high. Most opera is sung in its original language with digital surtitles in Czech. (Performances of works by Czech composers such as Dvořák and Smetana, for example, do not have surtitles in foreign languages.)

The National Theatre Ballet frequently performs ballet classics such as *Swan Lake* and *Coppélia*, but has been branching out in more adventurous directions in recent years by including choreographies by George Balanchine and Jiří Kylián.

The Ballet Company of the Prague State Opera is a recently formed, medium-sized company, incorporating the Prague Chamber Ballet. Its performances have been receiving excellent notices in the local press.

Jazz

Prague has long had a select but lively jazz scene, with a number of decent

clubs that at times attract respected foreign artists. However, there are also several excellent local players who can be seen nightly at the city's clubs, notably bass-player Tomáš Liška, jazz pianist Emil Viklický and guitarist Luboš Andršt.

THEATRE

Theatre in Prague has a long and venerable tradition – as might be expected in the capital of a country that, in 1989, chose a playwright as its first post-Communist president. There is still a lively theatrical scene in Prague, but, unless you are fluent in Czech, little will be accessible.

Probably of more interest to non-Czech speakers – and to children – are Prague's puppet theatres and the so-called 'Black Light' theatre developed for the 1958 World Expo. The most popular puppet show uses Josef Skupka's time-honoured characters of Spejbl and his son Hurvínek, and there are avant-garde, highly original performances as well. A good place to watch a performance is the National Marionette Theatre; Žatecká 1; tel: 224 819 322; www. mozart.cz.

During performances of Black Light theatre – the most famous company is at the Laterna magika – films and slides are projected onto multiple screens while actors, dressed completely in black to render them invisible, perform on stage, accompanied by a clever play of coloured lights. A certain amount of acrobatic skill is also often required of the actors.

NIGHTLIFE

Prague is no leading centre of nightlife in the way that London, Berlin or New York are, but it is still endeavouring to hold its own against smaller European capital cities. Generally, it's a good idea to avoid the places in the Wenceslas Square area, which tend to attract either mobs of teenage tourists or a rather seedy crowd; most locals won't go near such places. The better clubs are sprinkled all over the city, and there is no one best area for nightlife. Up-to-date listings can be found on the Czech-language site www.techno.cz.

Above from far left: Rudolfinum by night; ballet at the State Opera; the atmospheric Agharta jazz centrum jazz club (see p.122); pediment of the State Opera.

Czech Cinema

Films have been made at the Barrandov Studios in southern Prague since 1932, and in their first decade up to 80 films a year were made. During World War II, the studios were confiscated by the Nazis, who exploited the facilities to make propaganda films. After the war, the studios were nationalised and remained under state ownership until the 1990s. A new wave of Czech cinema occurred from 1963 to 1968, achieving international acclaim. Films such as *Closely Watched Trains* (Jiří Menzel) and *The Shop on Main Street* (Klos and Ján Kadár) won Oscars, and Miloš Forman's *The Firemen's Ball* and *Loves of a Blonde* were nominated. After the Soviet clampdown in 1968, many directors chose to emigrate and established themselves abroad. After the Velvet Revolution in 1989 the difficulties in adapting to the free market nearly led to the studios' bankruptcy in 2000. However, the dramatic decline in the number of Czech films was gradually compensated for by the increase in foreign productions, particularly those made by US producers, including such blockbusters as *Mission Impossible* (1996), *The Bourne Identity* (2002) and *Casino Royale* (2006).

HISTORY: KEY DATES

From the early Přemyslids to the Hussites and Habsburgs, through the early Republic, Fascism, Communism and then into the EU, Prague's history is long and complex, and has built the fascinating mix that is the contemporary city.

EARLY PERIOD TO THE PŘEMYSLID DYNASTY

Above from left:
Starting Work, displayed at the Ceremonial Hall, in Josefov; Art Nouveau stained-glass window by Alfons Mucha, St Vitus's Cathedral.

*c.*400 BC	Invasion by the Celtic Boii, from whom 'Bohemia' is derived.
AD 500s	Arrival of the Slavs.
900–1306	Rule of the Přemyslid dynasty; building of Prague Castle.
935	Prince Wenceslas, patron saint of Bohemia, is murdered by his brother Boleslav I.
1004	Bohemia comes under the jurisdiction of the Holy Roman Empire as Jaromír of Bohemia takes Prague with the aid of a German army.
1306	King Wenceslas II is assassinated, ending the Přemyslid dynasty.

THE GOLDEN AGE TO THE HUSSITE WARS

1310	King John of Luxembourg begins a new dynasty.
1348–78	Reign of King Charles I (later Emperor Charles IV); building of Charles Bridge.
1398–1415	Jan Hus preaches religious reform and is burnt at the stake.
1419	The 'first defenestration' of Prague begins the Hussite Wars, which continue intermittently for a century.

HABSBURG RULE

1526	Jagiellon King Louis is killed at the Battle of Mohács in Hungary; the throne passes to the Habsburgs.
1576	Emperor Rudolf II moves the Habsburg court to Prague.
1609	Rudolf's Letter of Majesty grants freedom of religious worship.
1618	Archduke Ferdinand tears up the Letter of Majesty. The 'second defenestration' of Prague prompts the Thirty Years War.
1620	Catholic victory under Emperor Ferdinand at Battle of the White Mountain. The Protestant 'Winter King', Frederick of the Palatinate, flees. Repression against Protestants results in mass exile.
1680	Bohemian peasants revolt against the feudal government.
1740	War of the Austrian Succession: the armies of Bavaria, Saxony and France capture Prague. Maria Theresa becomes empress.

1757	Seven Years War: Prussian forces bombard Prague. Maria Theresa has the castle extended and the damage to the city repaired.
1781	Joseph II abolishes serfdom; Prague's Jewish citizens are awarded civic rights. The ghetto is renamed Josefov.
1787	Première of Mozart's *Don Giovanni*.
1845	Arrival of the railway. The Industrial Revolution draws in Czechs from the countryside, diluting the German character of the city.
1848	Nationalist revolution in Prague crushed by the Austrians.
1880s	The Czech National Theatre opens. Composers Smetana, Dvořák and, later, Janáček gain international recognition.

INDEPENDENCE, THEN FASCISM, THEN COMMUNISM

1915	Tomáš Garrigue Masaryk goes into exile and gains Allied support for a new state uniting Czechs and Slovaks.
1918	Independent Republic of Czechoslovakia proclaimed. Masaryk becomes the first president, Edvard Beneš Foreign Minister.
1938	Munich Agreement cedes the Sudetenland to Hitler.
1939–45	Nazi occupation.
1945	Prague liberated by the Resistance and the Red Army. Almost all of Czechoslovakia's 2.7 million Germans are expelled.
1948	Communist coup replaces President Beneš with Communist leader Klement Gottwald.
1968	Prague Spring: an attempt to introduce 'socialism with a human face' under Party Secretary General Alexander Dubček. Attempt is crushed by a Warsaw Pact invasion.
1969	Dubček dismissed and 'normalisation' – a return to Stalinist orthodoxy – is overseen by party leader Gustav Husák.

THE POST-COMMUNIST ERA

1989	The 'Velvet Revolution' ends the Communist era. Václav Havel is elected president.
1993	The 'Velvet Divorce' creates separate Czech and Slovak republics.
2002	Prague suffers severe flooding.
2003	Havel is succeeded as president by Václav Klaus.
2004	The Czech Republic joins the European Union (EU).
2006	Following inconclusive elections, the country survives seven months without a government.
2007	US proposals for locating anti-missile defences on Czech soil cause bitter controversy.

Defenestrations
Czech history is strewn with defenestrations (the act of throwing someone out of a window). The tradition began in 1419 when the Hussites threw seven Catholic councillors from the New Town Hall, an act that sparked off the Hussite Wars. It continued in 1618 when two imperial councillors and their secretary were thrown from Prague Castle. Miraculously, they landed on a heap of manure and survived, though this time the outrage sparked off the Thirty Years War. In 1948, Jan Masaryk, the Foreign Minister – and one of the few non-Communists still in government – was found dead, dressed only in his pyjamas, in the courtyard of the Foreign Ministry, below his bathroom window. Investigations by the Communist authorities in 1948 and 1968 and a third one in the 1990s after the Velvet Revolution all came to the conclusion of death by suicide. A police investigation in 2004, however, concluded that he had been defenestrated by political opponents.

WALKS AND TOURS

PRAGUE CASTLE

The history of Prague began with the construction of the castle in the 9th century. Its attractive mix of palaces, churches, museums, gardens and galleries gives a fascinating insight into the origins of the city.

DISTANCE 1km (⅔ mile)
TIME A full day
START Black Tower
END Belvedere
POINTS TO NOTE

Although this route only covers a short distance, there is a lot to pack in, as it includes many of Prague's most important sights. Try to avoid the weekend crowds, especially during summer, but as one of Europe's major tourist attractions Prague Castle is busy year-round.

Above from far left: view of the castle in winter; fountain detail; old-fashioned lamp at the castle; smart, disciplined guards.

Prague Castle, or Pražský hrad *(for opening times, see box, below right)*, sprawls across the district known as Hradčany. Set on a hill overlooking the city, it is Prague's most impressive sight, especially when illuminated at night. More than 1,000 years old, it was the residence of the early Přemyslid rulers, who did well to establish their headquarters in this strategic position over the Vltava. Generations of rulers continued to expand the complex with churches and palaces, defensive and residential buildings. It is also the centre of spiritual power in

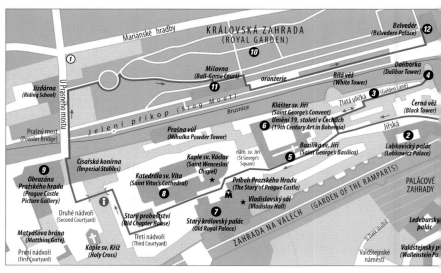

the city, as the site of the cathedral of St Vitus, and it retains its link with temporal power as the residence of the president of the Czech Republic.

OLD CASTLE STEPS

Begin at Malostranská metro station or the neighbouring tram stop. Turn left out of the station and walk up the hill, crossing Valdštejnská. This brings you to the bottom of the Old Castle Steps.

Black Tower and Lobkowicz Palace

Now lined with hawkers selling postcards, paintings and bijoux of dubious use, the steep climb brings you up to the **Black Tower ❶** (Černá věž), entrance to the castle proper. From the rampart just outside the gate there is a lovely view across the city.

Passing through the gate on the left is the entrance to the **Lobkowicz Palace ❷** (Lobkovický palác; tel: 602 595 998; www.lobkowiczevents.cz; daily 10.30am–6pm; charge). Previously in the hands of the state, this building was returned to the Lobkowicz family and is now home to their private art collection. The star exhibit is Pieter Brueghel the Elder's *Haymaking,* but there are also manuscripts by Mozart and Beethoven as well as a large display of armour.

Golden Lane

Further up Jiřská and to the right is the entrance to the attractive **Golden Lane ❸** (Zlatá ulička), one of the most popular – and crowded – attractions of the castle. It is said that Rudolf II housed his alchemists in these tiny houses, and Franz Kafka lived for a

Above: Basilica of St George; stained glass Rose Window at St Vitus's Cathedral.

Castle Tickets

Tickets for entry to the castle buildings are sold in the Third Courtyard in the Information Centre of Prague Castle (Informační středisko pražského hradu; tel: 224 373 368; www.hrad.cz). Two different types of ticket are available: a long tour version and a short tour ticket, both of which are valid for two days. They both cover the Old Royal Palace, the Story of Prague Castle, St George's Basilica, St George's Convent (housing the National Gallery's collection of 19th-century Bohemian art), Golden Lane and Daliborka Tower, the Castle Picture Gallery and the Powder Tower. The buildings are open daily, Apr–Oct 9am–6pm, Nov–Mar 9am–4pm. Entry to St Vitus is free, but note that you usually have to queue to get in, as visitor numbers are regulated.

Operatic Tales
The Dalibor Tower
is the setting
for Smetana's
nationalist opera
Dalibor, inspired
by the imprisonment
of Duke Dalibor
in the tower during
the 15th century.
According to
legend, the music
he made while
locked up was
so exquisite it
attracted crowds
of people to the
foot of the tower.

while at No. 22. At the end of the lane is the **Dalibor Tower** ❹ (Daliborka), part of the castle wall.

St George's Basilica

Jiřská ends at Náměstí sv. Jiří (St George's Square). Immediately on the right is **St George's Basilica** ❺ (Bazilika sv. Jiří), the oldest church still standing in the castle complex. It was founded in about AD 920 and rebuilt after a fire in the 12th century. Despite later alterations, the church has largely retained its Romanesque appearance. To the right of the choir is the Ludmilla Chapel, housing the tomb of the saint, the grandmother of Prince Wenceslas.

The church was part of a large monastic complex and the convent buildings next door now house the National Gallery's collection of **19th-Century Art in Bohemia** ❻ (Umění 19. století v Čechách). These lesser-known artists produced some very fine works, in particular the landscapes by Josef Navrátil, August Piepenhagen and Antonín Mánes.

OLD ROYAL PALACE

Dominating Náměstí sv. Jiří is the large bulk of St Vitus's Cathedral. However, ignore this for the moment and pass through the arch between church and buildings to the left, and turn sharp left to find the entrance to the **Old Royal Palace** ❼ (Starý královský palác).

An anteroom opens on to the **Vladislav Hall** (Vladislavský sál), named after King Vladislav II. This imposing late-Gothic throne room was built by the architect Benedikt Ried between 1493 and 1502.

On the same level, to the right, is the Bohemian Chancellery. It was from here that the imperial ambassadors were 'defenestrated' in 1618, sparking off the Thirty Years War. At the far end of the Vladislav Hall is a balcony overlooking the interior of All Saints Chapel, and the staircase that leads up from a doorway in the left-hand wall of the hall brings you to the New Land Records Office. This is decorated with the heraldic emblems of the Land Rolls officials on the ceiling and walls. The exit to the palace rooms takes you down the Riders' Staircase, built to allow rulers and guests to enter on horseback.

The lowest Gothic levels of the palace are now home to the exhibition **The Story of Prague Castle** (www.pribeh-hradu.cz). This informative display is particularly good for children and is in two parts: the first one leads you from room to room describing the development of the castle in chronological order; the second tells the 'Story of …' various subjects, such as residences, learning, burials, the Church and patronage.

ST VITUS

Continue around the cathedral to the main entrance at its western end. **St Vitus's Cathedral** ❽ (Katedrála sv. Víta; tel: 257 531 622; www.katedrala praha.cz; Mar–Oct: Mon–Sat 9am–5pm, Sun noon–5pm, Nov–Feb: Mon–Sat 9am–4pm, Sun noon–4pm; free) is the largest church in Prague, the

Above from far left:
Golden Lane; interior
of the Basilica of St
George; tunnel at the
castle; door detail.

metropolitan church of the Archdiocese of Prague, the royal and imperial burial church and also the place where the royal regalia are kept. Steeped in history, it was founded in 1344. Charles IV employed the French Gothic architect Matthew of Arras, and, when he died after eight years, the work was taken over by Petr Parléř. Construction was interrupted in the first half of the 15th century by the Hussite Wars. The cathedral was to remain incomplete until the 1860s, when a Czech patriotic association, following the old plans, completed the building in 1929.

Wenceslas Chapel

Aside from the magnificent vaulting in Parléř's splendid nave, the jewel in the crown of the cathedral is the **Wenceslas Chapel**. Built by Parléř on the South Transept, it is where the national saint Wenceslas was interred, and the walls are covered with frescoes and precious stones. A little door leads to the Treasure Chamber directly above the chapel. Here the Bohemian royal regalia are kept, behind seven locks, the seven keys of which are held by seven separate institutions.

PICTURE GALLERY

Leave the cathedral and carry on through the archway immediately opposite the exit. This brings you to the Third Courtyard of the castle. By now you will probably be feeling in need of refreshment, so turn left and take the archway out over the bridge (the Powder Bridge, or Prašný most)

that leads away from the castle: here is the restaurant **Lví Dvůr**, see ⑪①.

After eating, retrace your steps to the entrance to the Third Courtyard. On your right is the **Prague Castle Picture Gallery ❾** (Obrazárna Pražského hradu) This small but valuable collection was put together by Rudolf II, and although it has been plundered over the years, there are still some notable works by Rubens, Tintoretto, Titian and Veronese on display.

ROYAL GARDEN AND BELVEDERE

Cross back over the bridge and then turn right into the **Royal Garden ❿** (Královská zahrada). These are home to two important Renaissance buildings. The first you come to is the **Ball-Game Court ⓫** (Míčovna), built in 1565–9 and with a sgraffito façade. On the lower level beside the court is a modern greenhouse designed by the architect Eva Jiřičná, while at the end of the gardens is the **Belvedere ⓬** (Belvedér), built in 1537 as a summer palace.

Colourful Windows
In St Vitus look out for the window in the third chapel on the left. It was designed by Alfons Mucha, who is perhaps best known outside the Czech Republic for his Art Nouveau posters featuring the actress Sarah Bernhardt.

Food and Drink 🍴
① **LVÍ DVUR**
U Prašného mostu 6; tel: 224 372 361; daily 11am–midnight; €€
Previously the castle menagerie and now a decent restaurant, with a small outdoor café, with views over the cathedral and the palace gardens from its terrace. The food is mostly hearty and Czech along the lines of roast pork and dumplings, although there are a few lighter, Italian-inspired dishes.

NATIONAL GALLERY TO THE LORETA

Away from the bustle of the castle, Hradčany reveals itself as one of the most pleasant parts of the city, with delightful lanes to explore, churches and two major sites of the National Gallery collections.

Above from left:
Archbishop's Palace; frescoes on the ceiling of the cloisters at the Loreta; finely decorated walls of the Schwarzenberg Palace.

DISTANCE 1km (⅔ mile)
TIME A half-day
START Hradčanské náměstí
END The Loreta
POINTS TO NOTE

A much quieter route than the one through the castle grounds, but no less interesting. For those who have the energy – it would make for a long day – you could break route 1 at the castle's Third Courtyard and continue onto Hradčanské náměstí, the starting point of route 2.

Below: the Loreta.

Beyond the castle, Hradčany stretches up to the top of Petřín Hill. In between are atmospheric backstreets, imposing Renaissance and Baroque palaces, a couple of which are now important art galleries, as well as Prague's holiest pilgrimage site.

HRADČANY SQUARE

Climb up the steep road of Nerudova from Malostranské náměstí and at the top turn right onto Ke Hradu, a switchback that will bring you out onto **Hradčany Square ❶** (Hradčanské náměstí). This large open space leads, on one side, into the castle via the Matthais Gate, and in the other direction towards the Loreto Church and Strahov Monastery. In the centre of the square is an ornate Art Nouveau lamppost, somewhat out of place in the Renaissance and Baroque surroundings.

National Gallery

With your back to the castle, on the right-hand side of the square is the **Archbishop's Palace** (Arcibiskupský palác), dating from the 16th century but with a delightful mid-18th-century Rococo façade. Pass through the left-hand gateway of the palace and

take the passage leading downhill to the **Šternberg Palace** ❷ (Šternberský palác). This houses the National Gallery's collection of **European Painting from the Classical Era to the End of the Baroque** (tel: 233 090 570; www.ngprague.cz; Tue–Sun 10am–6pm; charge). Although the collection is neither large nor balanced it does contain some exceptional works. Chief among these are: the *Festival of the Rosary* (1506) by Albrecht Dürer; the two-sided *Hohenburg Altar* (1509) by Hans Holbein the Elder; Rembrandt's *The Scholar in His Study* (1634); and a portrait of *Eleonora of Toledo* (1540–3) by Bronzino. On the ground floor, opening onto the courtyard, is a pleasant café where you can have a quick coffee – and perhaps a cake – before carrying on.

Schwarzenberg Palace

Opposite the Archbishop's Palace is the sgraffito façade of the Renaissance **Schwarzenberg Palace** ❸ (Schwarzen bersky palác). This has been beautifully renovated and is now home to the National Gallery's collection of **Baroque Art in Bohemia** (tel: 233 081 713; www.ngprague.cz; Tue–Sun 10am–6pm; charge). There are three floors of galleries, and you start with the paintings on the top two (avoid the lift if you suffer from vertigo), with sculpture on the ground floor. Among the outstanding works are *Forest Stream* by Roe lant Savery and portraits by Petr Brandl.

LORETA SQUARE

Turn left out of the Schwarzenberg and walk up Loretánská to Loreta Square (Loretánské náměstí). As you turn right into the square on your left is the long façade of the **Černín Palace** (Černínský palác). The construction of the building, now home to the Czech Foreign Ministry, was so lavish that it made Emperor Leopold I jealous.

The Loreta

Opposite the palace is one of Prague's most important religious complexes,

Above: Loreta stonework details.

Multiple National Gallery Sites
The collections of Prague's National Gallery are spread out over several different sites: the Old Masters are in the Šternberg Palace; Baroque art is held opposite in the Schwarzenberg; art from the Middle Ages is on display in the Convent of St Agnes; 19th-centry art is spread between St George's Convent and the Kinský Palace; the House of the Black Madonna is dedicated to Czech Cubism; 20th- and 21st-century can be seen in the Trade Fair Palace; and, finally, the holdings of Asian art are in the Zbraslav Château just outside the city.

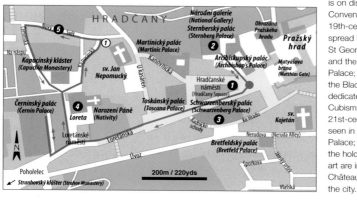

Above: decorative stone cherub on the Loreta.

Golden Glow
Many of the houses in Nový Svět have names displayed on house signs, and most include the adjective 'golden', a Prague tradition. Look out for the the 'Golden Leg', the 'Golden Star' and the 'Golden Pear' *(see Food and Drink box below right).*

the **Loreta** ❹ (Lorentánské námešti 7; tel: 220 516 740; www.loreta.cz; Tue–Sun 9am–12.15pm, 1–4.30pm; charge). The original Loreto is a place of pilgrimage in Italy. In the 13th century, angels are reputed to have brought the Casa Santa, the 'holy house' in which the Archangel Gabriel announced the birth of Jesus to Mary, from the Holy Land to the Italian village of Loreto. Over the years, the Italian Loreto cult became popular in Bohemia, and Habsburg rulers found this legend well suited to their purpose of returning heretical Hussites to the true faith. They therefore set about building more than 50 replicas of the 'holy house' across the land; the best-known of these is this one in Prague.

Between 1626 and 1750, a large complex of buildings was thrown up here, including a chapel, multi-storeyed cloisters, the Church of the Nativity, and an early Baroque tower with a carillon that dates back to 1694. In the courtyard is the Casa Santa (Svatá chyse) itself, built in 1626 by Giovanni Battista Orsi. Most visitors will find the Treasury *(see box)* the most memorable part of their visit, but don't miss the somewhat over-restored but still amusing frescoes in the cloisters.

NOVÝ SVĚT

Turn right out of the Loreta and take Kapuchinská, the small street that runs to the right from the bottom of the square. At the end of Kapuchinská turn left and you will find yourself in **Nový Svět** ❺. This line of tiny houses is one of the most attractive streets in Hradčany. Although it is now quite desirable, it was once rather run-down and mired in poverty, although several famous people have lived here; no. 1, the 'Golden Horn' (U zlatého rohu), was once home to the astronomer Tycho Brahe. If you are now feeling hungry, or in need of a rest, **U Zlaté hrušky**, see ❶❶, at no. 3 is a good place to stop.

The Treasure Chamber

The Loreta's main attraction is the Treasure Chamber. As in other places of pilgrimage, pilgrims over the years have given votive gifts to the treasury as a sign of thanksgiving. The gifts of the Bohemian nobility were commissioned from notable goldsmiths of the time and include some of the most valuable works of liturgical art in Central Europe. The most remarkable is the diamond monstrance, which was a legacy of Ludmilla Eva Franziska of Kolowrat. The monstrance, made in 1699 by Baptist Kanischbauer and Matthias Stegner of Vienna to a design by Johann Bernard Fischer von Erlach, is studded with 6,222 diamonds and sends out its rays like the sun. It measures almost 1m (3ft) in height and weighs more than 12kg (26lbs).

Food and Drink
① U ZLATÉ HRUŠKY
Nový Svět 3; tel: 220 514 778; daily 11.30am–3pm, 6.30pm–1am; €€€
The 'Golden Pear' is an attractive restaurant on one of Hradčany's loveliest streets. The building has been renovated and is very comfortable, while the menu is a good mix of international and Czech dishes, including, fittingly, pear soup with cinnamon gnocchi and roast duck.

STRAHOV MONASTERY AND PETŘÍN HILL

From the confines of the Strahov Monastery, stroll out onto the verdant slopes of Petřín Hill and enjoy panoramic views of the city from the observation tower, or else views of the sky from the observatory.

The route begins at Pohořelec, the square at the southwestern corner of Hradčany (the Castle District). On the south side of the square, go through the passage between the shops at no. 8 to enter the precinct of the Strahov Monastery. Alternative access is via the path that leads off Úvoz just nearby – where, if you start your walk around midday, you can also have lunch before you begin, see ⑪①.

> **DISTANCE** 2km (1¼ miles)
> **TIME** 2–3 hours
> **START** Pohořelec
> **END** Újezd
> **POINTS TO NOTE**
> Trams nos 22 and 23 stop at Pohořelec. Further along its route, tram no. 22 also stops near the bottom of the funicular railway on Újezd.

Above: the Strahov.
Below: Strahov railings and statue.

STRAHOV MONASTERY

The **Strahov Monastery** ❶ (Strahovský klášter, Strahovské nádvoří 1; tel: 233 107 749; www.strahovsky klaster.cz) was established by King Vladislav II in 1140 for the Premonstratensian Order. It is the oldest monastery in Bohemia and has had an eventful history. It was burnt down in 1258, damaged in the Hussite and Thirty Years wars and by a French bombardment in 1742, and was occupied by the Prussian army in the decades that followed. In 1952, all religious orders in Czechoslovakia were dissolved by the Communist authorities and it became a museum of literature. In 1990, though, the monks reclaimed their home and can be seen once again in thoughtful perambulation around the fruit trees of Petřín Hill.

Monastery Church
At the centre of the complex is the Church of the Annunciation of Our Lady (Nanebevzetí Panny Marie),

> ## Food and Drink ⑪
> **① MALÝ BUDDHA**
> Úvoz 46; tel: 220 513 894; Tue–Sun noon–10.30pm; €€
> Bizarre and incongruous it may be, but this is one of the better-value restaurants in tourist-thronged Hradčany, and a relaxing haven. This candlelit oriental teahouse serves good, mostly vegetarian food (spring rolls, noodles, Thai curries), as well as numerous varieties of tea, and ginseng wine.

St Roch
Enter the Strahov precinct by the west gate and you are greeted by the Church of St Roch (chrám sv. Rocha), patron saint of plague victims. It was commissioned by Rudolf II in 1603 after Prague had narrowly escaped an epidemic. It is now used for modern art exhibitions.

Above from left:
street near the
Strahov Monastery;
Theological Hall;
monastery spire;
Philosophical Hall.

which, although substantially remodelled by Anselmo Lurago in 1750, retains elements of the original Romanesque basilica built in 1143. Much of the decorative work you see today was executed by the Czech artist Jiří Neunhertz and depicts scenes from the life of St Norbert, Archbishop of Magdeburg and founder of the Premonstratensian Order in northern France in 1120. His remains were brought here in 1627 and interred in the chapel of St Ursula on the left of the nave. The church's organ was played by Mozart on at least two occasions.

Library

The monastery's main attraction for visitors today, though, is the **Library** – one of the most beautiful and extensive in the country (daily 9am–noon, 1–5pm; charge). The collection was established at the time of the foundation over 800 years ago, and the two halls on view to the public now house some 130,000 volumes, while a further 700,000 volumes are in storage. On the façade of the library building is a medallion featuring the portrait of Emperor Joseph II, who, in support of the Enlightenment, dissolved the majority of Bohemia's monasteries in 1783, though spared the Strahov. The Premonstratensians escaped dissolution by presenting their foundation as being primarily educational, and took advantage of the misfortune of other monasteries by acquiring many valuable collections. Further additions from the libraries of defunct monasteries came after World War II.

Inside, the first of the two library halls is the **Philosophers' Hall** (Filozofický sál), built by Ignaz Palliardi in 1782–4. The gilded walnut fittings came from the Bruck Monastery near Znojmo, which had just been dissolved. The Rococo ceiling fresco is

the work of Franz Anton Maulbertsch and was completed in only six months. It shows the development of humanity through wisdom, in tune with the prevailing Enlightenment ethos. At the two narrow ends you can see Moses with the tablets of law, and opposite, St Paul preaches at the pagan altar. The figure of Divine Providence is enthroned in the centre. On the longer sides of the hall are the great figures of history, from Adam and Eve to the Greek philosophers who made progress possible through their words and deeds.

The second hall is the **Theologians' Hall** (Teologický sál), built by Giovanni Domenico Orsi in 1671–9 in a rich Baroque style at a cost of 2,254 guilders. The frescoes were painted by Siardus Nosecký, a member of the Order, between 1723 and 1727. The theme is true wisdom, rooted in the knowledge of God. One of the cabinets lining the walls is barred: it contains books once banned by Church censors. In the middle of the room stand a number of valuable astronomical globes from the Netherlands, dating from the 17th century.

On display just outside the hall is a facsimile of one of the library's prize possessions, the 10th-century Strahov Gospel Book. In a bookcase nearby is the *Xyloteka* (1825), a set of books describing different tree species. Each book is bound in the wood and bark of a different tree, with samples of leaves, roots, flowers and fruits inside.

In the passage between the two libraries are cabinets of curiosities, mostly sea creatures from the collection of Karel Jan Erben, acquired by the monastery in 1798. Among the exhibits is a faked chimera and two whales' penises (next to the model ship and narwhal tusk). There is also a case containing a miniature coffee service

Below: the magnificent library.

PETŘÍN

Strahov Stadium

On the other (west) side of Petřín Hill from Malá Strana is the enormous Strahov Stadium (Velký Strahovský Stadión), built in the 1920s to designs by Alois Dryák. It was used by the Czech nationalist Sokol (or 'Falcon') movement for mass gymnastic displays. The movement's gatherings were later banned by the Communist authorities because of the undesirable similarities to organisations in Nazi Germany and because of its propagation of nationalist aspirations. The Sokol movement has since, however, been reformed.

made for the Habsburg empress Marie Louise in 1813, which fits into four false books.

Art Museum

The newly renovated **Strahov Collection of Art** (Tue–Sun 9am–noon, 12.30–5pm; charge) can be found in the second courtyard, accessed behind the monastery church. The works of art are mostly religious, though there are also secular works by Baroque and Rococo painters, including Norbert Grund (1717–67) and Franz Anton Maulbertsch (1724–96). One of the most important works on display is the wooden *Strahov Madonna*, by a mid-14th-century Czech sculptor. There is also a wonderful *Judith* from the workshop of Lucas Cranach the Elder (1472–1553).

Miniature Museum

A final attraction within the monastery precinct is the **Miniature Museum** (Strahovské nádvoří 11; tel: 233 352 371; daily 9am–5pm; charge). Here you can observe the handiwork of Siberian technician Anatoly Konyenko with the aid of microscopes arranged around the walls of two small rooms. Mr Konyenko used to manufacture tools for eye microsurgery, but has since diverted his talents to inscribing a prayer on a human hair, creating images of cars on the leg of a mosquito, fashioning a pair of horseshoes for a flea and making the world's smallest book.

PETŘÍN HILL

Leaving the monastery by the east gate, you emerge onto **Petřín Hill** (Petřínské sady) The park was formed by linking up the gardens that had gradually replaced vineyards and a quarry (which provided the stone for the city's buildings). Turn right along the path, with the fruit trees on the slopes to your left, and when you come to some flights of steps, turn right for the final ascent to the top of the hill.

Observation Tower

At the top, there is a café (and toilets), where you can recuperate. Then, when you are ready, there are 299 more steps to climb, this time up the **Observation Tower ❷** (Rozhledna; tel: 257 320 112; daily: Apr and Sept 10am–7pm, May–Aug 10am–10pm, Oct 10am–6pm, Nov–Mar Sat–Sun 10am–5pm; charge). This replica of the Eiffel Tower is, at 60m (197ft), only a fifth of the height of the original, but offers

---

Food and Drink

② SAVOY CAFÉ
Vítězná 5; tel: 257 311 562; Mon–Fri 8am–10.30pm, Sat–Sun 9am–10.30pm; €€
Smart and stylish café-restaurant that is good for breakfast, lunch, dinner or just coffee and cake. The menu includes fried eggs with black truffle, steak tartare, and cottage cheese dumplings stuffed with fruit.

③ THE OLYMPIA
Vítzná 7; tel: 251 511 080; daily 11am–midnight; €€
A restaurant has operated out of this building almost since it was built in 1903. The present incarnation is as a smart bar-restaurant licensed from the Pilsner Urquell Brewery. The emphasis of the menu is on comforting Czech butchery, goose, duck, sausages, pork hock, lamb knuckle, though it also extends to risotto, pasta and salads. The cooking is highly creditable, as is the value for money.

spectacular views of the city (and in good weather, even to the forests of Central Bohemia). It was constructed out of old railway tracks in 31 days for Prague's 1891 Jubilee Exhibition. During the Nazi occupation, however, Hitler wanted to have it removed because he felt it ruined the view from his room in the castle.

The Maze

Just beyond the tower, and also built for the 1891 Exhibition, is the **Mirror Maze** ❸ (Zrcadlová Bludiště; tel: 257 315 212; opening times as for the tower; charge). Popular with children, this cast-iron mock-Gothic castle has its own drawbridge and turrets. Inside is a hall of distorting mirrors as well as a wax diorama of the battle between the Praguers and the Swedes in 1648 on the Charles Bridge. Outside again, just opposite is the Church of St Lawrence (kostel sv. Vavřince), a Romanesque building with a Baroque façade.

The Observatory

Retracing your steps towards the tower, turn left through the opening in the massive wall. This is the so-called **Hunger Wall** (Hladová zed'), which was commissioned by Charles IV in 1362 as a form of 'New Deal' strategy to provide work for the starving and impoverished.

At this point, take the path to the left to make your way to the **Observatory** ❹ (Štefánikova hvězdárna; tel: 257 320 540; www. observatory.cz; opening times vary, but generally Tue–Fri 2–7pm, Sat–Sun 10am–noon, also 9–11pm during summer). During the day, the 1928 Zeiss telescope is trained on Mercury and Venus as well as sunspots; on clear nights it looks out at the moon, stars and planets.

FUNICULAR RAILWAY

To finish the route, retrace your steps back along the Hunger Wall to the station for the **Funicular Railway** ❺ (lanová dráha; www.dpp.cz; daily 9am–11.30pm; normal tram and metro tickets are valid). When first built in 1891, the train going up the hill was powered solely by the weight of the other one coming down – the cars had water tanks, which were filled at the top and emptied at the bottom. From the 1960s, however, the railway underwent reconstruction and finally reopened in 1985, powered by more modern means.

If, on reaching the bottom of the hill, you have worked up an appetite, turn right (south) on Újezd and turn left into Vítzná for the **Savoy Café** and **The Olympia**, see ⑪② and ⑪③.

Above from far left: sign on the funicular railway; the Observatory; Petřín Hill Observation Tower.

Wooden Church
On the south side of Petřín Hill is the little wooden church of St Michael (chrám sv. Michal), a wonderful example of 18th-century folk art. It comes from the Carpathian Ukraine and was rebuilt on this spot in 1929, a gift from the inhabitants of the small Ukrainian village of Mukacevo, which had become part of Czechoslovakia after World War I and was annexed by the Soviet Union after World War II. A belfry from Wallachia stands next to the church.

Villa Kinský

In the most southerly corner of the park on Petřín Hill is the Villa Kinský, now the Musaion (Kinského zahrada 98; www.nm.cz; May–Sept Tue–Sun 10am–6pm, Oct–Apr Tue–Sun 9am–5pm; charge) and a branch of the National Museum. It houses the ethnographic collection, with displays on traditional Czech folk culture and art, music, costume, farming methods and handicrafts. There are regular folk concerts and demonstrations of crafts such as blacksmithing and woodcarving.

CHARLES BRIDGE AND MALÁ STRANA

Occupying the slopes between the river and the castle, Malá Strana, or 'Lesser Town', constitutes the most intact Baroque townscape in Central Europe. Its cobbled streets and burghers' houses seem straight out of the pages of a fairy tale.

DISTANCE 4km (2½ miles)
TIME A full day
START Charles Bridge
END Kampa Park
POINTS TO NOTE
Start early in the morning to beat the crowds and see the bridge in the mist.

Above: Charles Bridge statues.

Malá Strana (Lesser Town) lies at the foot of Prague Castle, demarcated from the rest of the city by parks and the River Vltava. From humble beginnings in the 9th century, it was elevated to the status of a town in 1257 (the second-oldest of the five towns that originally formed Prague) by the Přemyslid ruler, Otakar II; merchants were invited from Germany to set up shop on the land beneath the castle walls.

It experienced its first boom during the reign of Charles IV (1346–78), when it was extended and received new fortifications. It then suffered major damage in the Hussite Wars in 1419, and in the Great Fire of 1541, when catastrophic damage necessitated a major rebuilding programme.

Malá Strana truly blossomed after the victory of the Catholic League over the Bohemians in the Battle of White Mountain in 1620, which concluded the Bohemian phase of the Thirty Years' War. In the redistribution of property that followed, many wealthy families loyal to the House of Habsburg settled here on the parcels of land they had received. Subsequently, the court moved back to Vienna and most of the palaces were then deserted. They were, however, kept intact and have been spared major alteration to this day. Even the town houses, which often have much older foundations, have retained their Baroque façades and characteristic house signs.

CHARLES BRIDGE

The route begins at the **Charles Bridge ❶** (Karlův most), commissioned by Charles IV 1357 to replace the earlier Judith Bridge, which collapsed in a flood in 1342. Completed *c.*1400, it was built by Petr Parléř (who also designed St Vitus's Cathedral) and has withstood centuries of traffic and numerous floods, thanks, so legend has it, to the use of eggs in the mortar.

Staré Město Side of the Bridge

On the Staré Město side of the bridge, is Parléř's **Old Town Bridge Tower** (Staroměstská mostecká věž; May–Oct daily 10am–10pm, winter closing times vary between 5pm and 7pm; charge). It was here that in 1648, at the end of the Thirty Years War, an army of Swedish invaders was fought off by a band of Prague townspeople. Despite being damaged in the fracas, much of the sculptural decoration has survived. Look on the external corners for the figures of 14th-century gropers feeling up buxom ladies.

Inside the tower is an uninspiring exhibition on the history of the building since its construction commenced in 1373. Your entrance fee is justified, however, by the fine views from the roof.

Crossing the bridge itself, you pass a succession of statues and monuments, the majority of which are copies of the Baroque originals. The earliest of these is a crucifix (third on the right) erected in 1657. In 1696, a Jewish man was found guilty of blaspheming in front of the crucifix and was made to pay for the gold Hebrew inscription that reads, 'Holy, Holy, Holy Lord God Almighty'.

The most famous statue on the bridge is that of **St John of Nepomuk** (eighth on the right), placed here in 1683. King Wenceslas IV was supposed to have had this priest killed after he refused to divulge the contents of the queen's confession; he was dressed up in a suit of armour and thrown over the side of the bridge.

Other important statues include that of **St Luitgard** (fourth from the end on the left), sculpted by Matthias Braun in 1710 and often considered the finest work on the bridge, and the **group**

Above from far left:
view of the Charles Bridge; military statue on the bridge; statue of St John of Nepomuk; bronze bas-relief depicting St John of Nepomuk being thrown off the bridge: note that the detail is smudged, where people have rubbed it for luck.

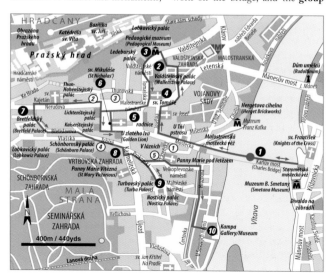

featuring **SS John of Matha and Félix de Valois**. In the 12th century, these two saints founded the Trinitarian Order in order to raise ransoms for crusaders captured by the Turks. Inexplicably, St Ivan has also gatecrashed the group.

Malá Strana Side of the Bridge

On the Malá Strana side of the bridge, to the right, on a lower level, is the **Ostriches Hotel** (U tří pštros ů; www.upstrosu.cz), with an old painting of three ostriches on the outside. In the late 16th century the building belonged to a merchant who supplied feathers to the crown. It then became a coffee house in 1714 and later a hotel (Goethe was one of its early guests).

Before entering Malá Strana, you first encounter two towers. The shorter one was originally part of the 12th-century **Judith Bridge** that preceded the Charles Bridge. The taller one (on the right) is the **Malá Strana Bridge Tower** (Malostranská mostecká věž; daily mid-Mar–Oct 10am–6pm; charge) and was built from 1464 in imitation of the tower on the Staré Město side of the bridge. Inside is an exhibition on the history of the bridge, though, again, it is the views from the top that justify the entrance fee.

Above: in the gardens at the Waldstein Palace.

NORTHERN MALÁ STRANA

Mostecká

Passing under the bridge tower, you come on to **Mostecká** (Bridge Street). If you are keen to take breakfast or a snack before continuing the walk, make a detour to **Bohemia Bagel**, see ⑪①, off to the left on Lázeňská.

Back on Mostecká, among the fine Baroque houses is the 18th-century Kaunitz Palace at no. 15, now the Serbian Embassy. Further up, turn right onto Josefská. At the end of the street on your right is the pretty Baroque Church of St Joseph, which, since 1989, has been restored to the Loreto Sisters (founded by Mary Ward in 1609).

Waldstein Palace and Gardens

Turning right onto Letenská, continue on until you find a doorway in the high wall on your left. This is the entrance to the gardens of the **Waldstein (or Wallenstein) Palace ②** (Valdštejnský palác; tel: 257 072 759; gardens Apr–Oct daily 10am–6pm, palace Sat–Sun 10am–4pm; free). This was the first Baroque palace in Prague, built 1624–30 by Italian architects for General Albrecht von Wallenstein (1583– 1634; *see margin right*). Take a stroll around the beautiful gardens before heading to the palace on the far side.

The gardens are overlooked by a triple-arched loggia *(sala terrena)*, decorated with frescoes of scenes from the Trojan War. It was here that Wallenstein dined during the 12 months he lived in the palace.

Food and Drink 🍴

① BOHEMIA BAGEL
Lázeňská 19; tel: 257 218 192; daily 7.30–11pm; €–€€
Dependable American-style café, serving fresh bagels and sandwiches, cooked breakfasts (until 2pm), pancakes, muffins, salads, quiches and burgers. Free refills of coffee and soft drinks. Wine and beer also on offer. Internet access available.

On the western side of the gardens is a large aviary (home to several owls) and an extraordinary artificial grotto with stalactites and grotesques. Elsewhere around the garden are bronze statues of mythological figures – the work of Adriaen de Vries, court sculptor to Emperor Rudolf II. Unfortunately, these are only copies; the originals were taken to Sweden as spoils of war in 1648 and are now in the park of Drottningholm Palace near Stockholm. At the gardens' eastern end is a large ornamental pond and a former Riding School, where temporary exhibitions are held.

The palace itself matches Wallenstein's grand political ambitions and was intended to rival Prague Castle. Wallenstein was an enthusiastic acquirer of property (by 1625 he owned a quarter of all Bohemia) and bought up 26 houses and even a city gate to build this palace. Today it houses the Czech Senate, although various rooms are open to the public.

The main hall has ceiling paintings by Baccio di Bianca, which feature Wallenstein depicted as Mars, god of war, riding his chariot to battle. Next is the Knights' Hall, with its unusual 19th-century leather wall covering, and then the circular Audience Chamber and the Mythological Corridor, decorated with scenes from Ovid and Virgil.

Pedagogical Museum

Exit the Palace onto Valdštejnská and turn left. When you reach Waldstein Square, on your right is the **Pedagog-** ical Museum ❸ (tel: 257 533 455; Tue–Sat 10am–5pm; charge), which charts the development of education, based on the works of the Czech philosopher Comenius (1592–1670). Off the square to your left is Tomáška, continuing the tour.

Tomáška

Walking along Tomáška you pass several fine Baroque houses, including **The Golden Stag** and **The Golden Pretzel** (no. 12). These house signs date from the time before house numbers were introduced (in 1770 by Joseph II). They were based on the profession or craft of the house owner, his status or the immediate environment of the house. Animals and other symbolic signs, of both a secular and a religious nature, were popular. If the house owner changed, the house retained its original sign – and sometimes the new owner even took the name of the house himself.

St Thomas's Church

At the end of the street, on the left is **St Thomas's Church** ❹ (Kostel sv. Tomáše; Josefská 8; Mon–Sat 11am–1pm, Sun 9am–midday, 4.30–5.30pm). The church is the most impressive part of a former Augustinian monastery founded in the 13th century. Its present Baroque form (late 1720s) is the work of Kilián Ignaz Dientzenhofer. The church originally had two altarpieces by Rubens (the *Martyrdom of St Thomas* and *St Augustine*), now replaced by copies (the originals are in the National Gallery's Šternberg

Fortunes of War

Wallenstein enlisted under the Habsburg Ferdinand II in the Thirty Years War. He won many victories, became Duke of Mecklenburg, and accumulated great wealth (not least with a grandiose coin swindle). In the end he was able to raise his own private army, the services of which became so expensive that parts of the empire were mortgaged to afford them. He went too far, however, when he hatched a secret deal with the enemy that would eventually have led him to the Bohemian crown. Emperor Ferdinand saw through him: he hired assassins who murdered him in his bed in the town of Cheb in 1634.

More Gardens

There are two other gardens in the vicinity of the Waldstein that are also open to the public. At Valdštejnská 10 is the Kolowrat Palace (Kolowratský palác), whose terraced gardens are in the Italian style. Then on U lužického semináře, which runs parallel to Letenská to the south, is the entrance to Vojan Park, which contains two Baroque chapels and is often used to display modern sculptures.

Palace; *see p.31*). The ceiling frescoes are by the Bohemian artist Václav Vavřinec Reiner. Next door are cloisters and what was once the monastic brewery (founded in 1358). At the time of writing, its beer cellar was undergoing renovation.

Lesser Town Square

At the end of Tomáška is the **Lesser Town Square** ❺ (Malostranské náměstí). On the lower side of the square at no. 21 is the quarter's old town hall, while at no. 18 is the Smiřický Palace, where Protestant nobles planned the second Prague defenestration in 1618 *(see p.22)*. On the other (west) side

of the square is the **Lichtenstein Palace**, with its broad Classical façade. From 1620 to 1627 it belonged to Karl von Lichtenstein, the so-called 'Bloody Governor' who was mainly responsible for the execution of the leaders of the 1618 rebellion.

Nearby is the **Kaiserstein Palace**, which bears a plaque memorialising the opera singer Ema Destinová, who once lived there. On the south side of the square is the **Golden Lion House** at no. 10, one of the few purely Renaissance houses remaining in the Malá Strana.

St Nicholas's Church

Dominating the square is the **Church of St Nicholas** ❻ (Kostel sv. Mikuláše; tel: 257 534 215; www.psalterium.cz; Mar–Oct 9am–5pm, Nov–Feb 9am–4pm; charge), probably Prague's finest Baroque building and a potent symbol of the Counter-Reformation. It was started in the early 18th century by the Bavarian architect Christoph Dientzenhofer, who designed the façade, nave and side chapels. His son, Kilián Ignaz, added the choir and the dome, and then Anselmo Lurago completed the building with a tower in 1755. Except in winter, it is possible to ascend the **tower** (daily 10am–6pm) for fine views.

The church's newly restored interior features one of the largest ceiling frescoes in Europe in the nave. Painted by Johann Lukas Kracker in 1770, it portrays scenes from the life of St Nicholas. Meanwhile, the 75m (247ft) high dome is decorated with František Xaver Palko's *Celebration of the Holy*

Trinity. You can get a good view of the frescoes from the gallery above the nave (entrance via the steps lies to the left of the main altar). The gallery also displays Karel Škréta's *Passion* cycle (1673–4).

In front of the four pillars supporting the dome is a set of sculptures of the Eastern Church Fathers (executed 1755–69) by Ignác František Platzer. He was also responsible for the gilded statue of *St Nicholas* (1765) by the high altar designed by Andrey Pozza. The ornate pulpit is made of artificial marble and covered with gilt (from the workshop of R.J. Prachner, 1762–6). The church's 2,500-pipe organ, completed in 1746 before the building itself was finished, is supposed to have been played by Mozart in 1787. On his death in 1791, his famous *Requiem* was performed in the church as a tribute.

Outside again, the massive block next door is a former Jesuit College, while in the middle of the square is a plague column by Giovanni Alliprandi (1715). To continue the route, now make for the northwest corner of the square and Nerudova.

Nerudova

The street of Nerudova is named after the Czech poet and author Jan Neruda (1834–91), who lived in the upper part of the street, at no. 47, U dvou slunc ů (The Two Suns). His work, particularly *Tales of the Lesser Quarter*, was inspired by the everyday life of Malá Strana.

Before you walk up the street, stop off for refreshments at **U Kocoura** at no.

2 on your right, or else at **U Hrocha** on the street behind it, see ⑪② and ⑪③.

Many of the middle-class houses on Nerudova were originally built in a Renaissance style and later given Baroque façades. Most have house signs: **The Three Violins** (several generations of violin-makers lived here) at no. 12, **The Golden Chalice** at no. 16, **St John of Nepomuk** at no. 18 and **The Donkey and the Cradle** at no. 25. A pharmacy was formerly housed in **The Golden Lion** at no. 32.

Two embassies have settled into the Baroque palaces in this street. On the left at no. 5 is the **Morzin Palace** (built 1714), now the Romanian Embassy. Its façade is ornamented with the work of Ferdinand Maximilian Brokoff: Moors supporting the balcony, allegorical figures of Day and Night, and sculptures representing the four corners of the world. Further up at no. 20 is the Thun-Hohenstein Palace (built 1726) – now the Italian Embassy – and decorated (by Matthias Bernard Braun) with two eagles with outspread wings and statues of Jupiter and Juno.

Above from far left: the dome at St Nicholas's Church; Old Town restaurant; the view from Malá Strana.

Above: sun emblem decorating a house in the Lesser Town; cherub, St Thomas's.

Opposite below: St Thomas's Church.

Food and Drink 🍴

② U KOCOURA

Nerudova 2; tel: 257 530 107; daily 11am–11pm; €–€€
The Tomcat pub used to be owned by the Friends of Beer, which was once a political party, but now merely a civic association. Despite its location near Malostranské náměstí, its prices are very reasonable.

③ U HROCHA

Thunovské 20; tel: 222 516 978; daily 11am–11pm; €–€€
The Hippo is one of the few places in the district still aimed at local residents. Simple wooden furniture, a smoky atmosphere, excellent beer and basic high-carb food to soak up the alcohol.

St Mary Victorious

At Karmelitská 9 is the Church of St Mary Victorious (daily 8.30am–7pm). Begun in 1611, it was Prague's first, though by no means best, Baroque church. After the Battle of the White Mountain it was confiscated from the Protestants and became a stronghold of the Counter-Reformation. It is here that the famous Bambino di Praga is kept, a 16th–17th-century wax figure (of Spanish origin) of the infant Jesus, dressed in one of its 72 costly robes, some of which are on display in the upstairs museum. This little figure is revered by Catholic pilgrims, and is believed to work miracles.

Next to the palace is the **Church of Our Lady of Perpetual Succour**, which operated as a theatre from 1834 to 1837, presenting numerous plays during the Czech National Revival. On the other side of the road, Neruda's house at no. 47 has long since functioned as a pub. In the Communist era, it was a favourite meeting place for the Plastic People of the Universe, the underground rock band whose arrest prompted Václav Havel and others to found Charter 77, the petition against the governing regime's human rights violations.

SOUTHERN MALÁ STRANA

Below Nerudova

Retracing your steps a little, at no. 33 you will find the Rococo **Bretfeld Palace** ❼ (Bretfeldský palác) with a relief of St Nicholas on the portal. In earlier years lavish balls took place here, some of which Mozart and Casanova are said to have attended. Close by, the steps Jánský Vršek lead down the hillside. Look out for the turning off to the left onto Břetislavova, at the end of which turn right into Tržiště.

Continue past the 17th-century Schönborn Palace, which is now the heavily guarded US Embassy (all passing cars are stopped and searched), and on to no. 7: **Gitanes**, see ⑪④, a good place to stop for a hearty meal. At the end of the road, turn right.

Just around the corner on Karmelitská is the gate to the **Vrtba Gardens** ❽ (Vrtbovská zahrada; Apr–Oct daily 10am–6pm; charge). This World Heritage Site offers perhaps the finest example of Baroque landscaping in Prague. The garden contains a number of sculptures by Matthias Bernhard Braun and a pavilion with frescoes by Václav Vavřinec Reiner. On the other side of Karmelitská is the turning for Prokopská, which leads down to Maltézské náměstí.

Maltese Square

Maltese Square ❾ (Maltézské náměstí) takes its name from the fact that for centuries the Knights of Malta lived in the vicinity. In 1169, they founded a monastery just behind where the Gothic Church of Our Lady Beneath the Chain stands to this day, at the junction with Lázeňská. The 'chain' of the church's name is a reference to the barrier used by the knights to guard the Judith Bridge (since swept away by floods and replaced with the Charles Bridge). It is the oldest surviving church in Malá Strana, though the remains of its 12th-century Romanesque predecessor can still be seen in the right-hand wall of the forecourt. Opposite the church, on Lázeňská, is a useful place for a pitstop, see ⑪⑤.

Adjacent to the Church of St Mary Beneath the Chain is another square, **Velkopřevorské náměstí**. On one side is the **Buquoy Palace**, home of the French Embassy, and opposite is the former **Palace of the Grand Prior of the Knights of Malta**, one of the most beautiful in the area. The wall of the Palace of the Grand Prior, facing the French Embassy, is known as the John Lennon Wall.

During the 1980s, this graffiti-strewn wall was the focus of Prague's Beatles-worship. The 'mural', with its depiction of John Lennon, was twice under threat; first from the secret police, who painted it over, and then from the Knights of Malta, when it had been repainted and the property returned to them under the post-1989 restitution. The wall was finally saved from respectability by the intervention of the French ambassador, who appealed to the authorities to let it be.

Kampa Island

Continuing the route (with the wall on your left), go straight on at the cross-roads and over the small river – the Čertovka or Devil's Stream – onto **Kampa Island**. This little district is sometimes referred to as Little Venice on account of its situation, watermills and gardens. Turn right at the end of the road on to Hroznová and head south.

Much of the southern part of the island is given over to Kampa Park, a green space formed in 1940 by linking up the gardens of former palaces. Bounded by water on both sides, it has remained undeveloped because of the constant risk of flooding. Even so, no one was prepared for the severity of the flood of 2002. Fortunately, there is little evidence of the scale of the devastation.

Continue south through the park along U Lužickeho Seminář and then take the path off to your left towards the river bank and the **Kampa Museum** ❿ (Museum Kampa; tel: 257 286 147; daily 10am–6pm; www.museumkampa. cz; charge). The building is a converted watermill with several modern additions: a staircase leads up to a glass cube (by Marian Kasměla) on top of the building and excellent views. There is also a glass footbridge (by Czech artist Václav Cigler), which appears to lead you out over the river. The proximity of the river ensured, of course, that the museum was inundated by the 2002 floods. The large sculpture of a chair on the embankment outside was washed 40km (25 miles) downstream.

Based around the collections of wealthy Czech ex-pats Jan and Meda Mladek, the museum has large holdings of the works of the abstract painter František Kupka (1871–1963) and the Expressionist and Cubist sculptor Otto Gutfreund (1889–1927). A good portion of the exhibition space is given over to displays of contemporary Central European art.

Above from far left: Kampa Museum; John Lennon Wall; in a Kampa Island park; pretty riverside spot.

Lázeňská

The street of Lázeňská harbours several historic buildings. No. 6, The Spa (V lázních), functioned as a luxury hotel until the 19th century, with a guest list that included Tsar Peter the Great and, as a memorial plaque proclaims, the French poet François-René de Chateaubriand. At no. 11 is the house known as The Golden Unicorn (U zlatého jednorozce), which once played host to the composer Ludwig van Beethoven.

Food and Drink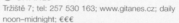

④ GITANES
Tržiště 7; tel: 257 530 163; www.gitanes.cz; daily noon–midnight; €€€
Cosy restaurant specialising in the cuisine of the former Yugoslavia. The atmosphere is set by the flowery cloths on the tables and Naïve paintings, photographs and farm implements on the walls. The menu completes the sense of nostalgia: home-made bread with paprika milk-fat spread, roasted chips made from salty dough, Javorina schnitzel, lamb sausages, pasta alla Trieste, Yugoslavian cheeses and boiled apples filled with nuts and topped with whipped cream.

⑤ CUKRKÁVALIMONÁDA
Lázeňská 7; tel: 257 530 628; daily 8.30am–8pm; €€
'Sugar-coffee-lemonade' is a beautifully styled café offering variations around scrambled eggs for breakfast, then pastas, frittatas, pancakes and sandwiches throughout the day, and then Mediterranean-style meals in the evening – salmon tagliatelle, chicken and prosciutto, trout and thyme. Try also the home-made pastries and cakes and speciality hot chocolate.

STARÉ MĚSTO

Staré Město, or the Old Town, has more to offer than just Baroque churches and cobbled streets. This route takes in an astronomical clock, a jewel thief's mummified arm, Mozart's theatre and an eccentric collection of tribal art.

DISTANCE 3km (2 miles)
TIME A full day
START Charles Bridge
END Bethlehem Square
POINTS TO NOTE

You may decide to do this walk in two instalments: first Western Staré Město and the Old Town Square, then Southern Staré Město.

Smetana Museum

On a small spit of land, just south of the Charles Bridge, is the Smetana Museum (Muzeum Bedřicha Smetany; tel: 222 220 082; Wed–Mon 10am–noon, 12.30–5pm; charge), dedicated to the nationalist composer Bedřich Smetana (1824–84). Housed in a neo-Renaissance former municipal waterworks, the museum illustrates the life and work of the father of Czech music with scores, diaries, manuscripts and his personal paraphernalia.

Staré Město, or the Old Town, is situated on the right bank of the Vltava. The pattern of its streets and squares has remained largely unaltered since the Middle Ages. Its perimeter is marked by streets that trace of the lines of the former city walls – Národní třída, Na příkopě and Revoluční.

Originally the Old Town lay some 2–3m (6–9ft) below the modern street level. The area, however, proved vulnerable to flooding, and consequently the street level has been raised little by little since the late 13th century. Many of the district's houses still have Romanesque rooms hidden in their basements.

WESTERN STARÉ MĚSTO

The walk begins by the Charles Bridge in Křižovnické náměstí (Knights of the Cross Square). The Knights of the Cross were founded as a crusader Order of monks in the early 13th century and established themselves here not long after. Since 1989, they have reclaimed their property on the northern side of the square.

Here can be found their domed Baroque Church of St Francis built by the French architect Jean-Baptiste Mathey from 1679 to 1685. Its ornate interior features frescoes by Václav Vavřinec Reiner and Jan Krystof Lisk. Next door, in the Order's former hospital, is the **Charles Bridge Museum** (tel: 739 309 551; daily 10am–8pm, winter until 6pm; charge). As well as an exhibition on the history of the bridge, you can see the foundations of the earlier Judith Bridge which was swept away by floods in 1342. There is also access here to an underground chapel adapted by Mathey from the vaults of an earlier Gothic church on the site. He decorated it in grotto style, with stalactites made out of dust and eggshells.

Clementinum

Across the road is the Baroque façade of St Salvator (completed in 1601, though modified by Carlo Lurago around 1650), part of the sprawling complex of the **Clementinum ❶** (Klementinum; grounds daily 6am–

11pm; free). This college was founded in 1556 by the Jesuits, who had been summoned to the country by the Habsburgs to spearhead the Counter-Reformation and cancel out the revolutionary ideas promulgated by the Protestant Karolinum University (of which Jan Hus had once been rector). As the Jesuits' wealth accrued, they bought up churches, gardens and 30 houses to extend their precinct.

In 1773, however, not long after the buildings were finally completed, Joseph II forced the Jesuits into exile in enthusiastic compliance with the Pope's decree to suppress the Order (it had become a political liability). Today, the Clementinum is part of Charles University and accommodates four libraries and a concert venue.

Enter by the gate just to the left of St Salvator. Cross the first courtyard and walk through the arch. Immediately on your left is the **National Library**, with its collection of 6 million volumes. On your right is the **Church of St Clement**, which is often open to the visitors. Its exuberant Baroque interior was designed by Kilián Dientzenhofer between 1711 and 1715. It now ministers to a Greek Orthodox congregation. Just behind it is the oval-shaped Italian Chapel, which can be seen from the street outside, but is closed to the public. Built around 1590 for the Italian craftsmen working in the complex, it is still technically owned by the Italian government.

At the far end of this second courtyard is the **Astronomical Tower** on your left. Entrance to the **Baroque Hall** is just beneath it, and entrance to both can be gained through one of the guided tours on offer (tel: 222 220 879; daily, tours on the hour from 10am, last tour at 7pm; charge). Tickets can be purchased at the **Mirrored Chapel** (which is also included

Above from far left:
close-up of the Astronomical Clock; Old Town rooftops.

Above: Clementinum; Old Town Square; Jan Hus statue.

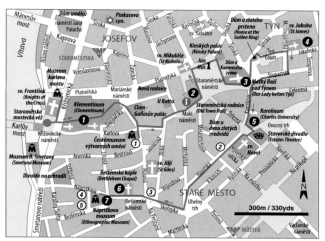

The Royal Way
On coronation day, this was the processional route followed by Czech kings on their way to St Vitus's Cathedral. Beginning at the Powder Tower, the king and his entourage proceeded along Celetná, through Old Town Square and Malé náměstí, along Karlova and across the Charles Bridge to Malostranské náměstí, before climbing up Nerudova to the castle.

in the tour) in the next courtyard, through the arch on the left.

The **Baroque Library Hall** was completed in 1722 and ever since has housed a collection of theological books (those with whitened backs and red marks date back to the Jesuit period). The allegorical ceiling frescoes by Jan Hiebl depict antique learning as the basis for Christian teachings. Above the library is the Astronomical Tower, also built in the 1720s and used for observation of the skies right up until the 1930s. Halfway up you can see the Prague meridian; when sunlight crossed the line at noon, a flag used to be hung from the tower and a cannon let off.

The **Chapel of Mirrors** is a frequent venue for concerts, during which you can gaze at Jan Hiebl's frescoed ceiling, with its strips that illustrate verses of the Hail Mary prayer, and Václav Vavřinec Reiner's murals of scenes from the life of the Virgin Mary. To exit the complex, walk through the gate to the far right-hand corner of the courtyard into Marianské náměstí.

Husova

On the south side of Marianské náměstí on the corner of Husova is the **Clam-Gallas Palace**. This magnificent Baroque building was constructed between 1713 and 1730 by the Viennese court architect, Johann Bernhard Fischer von Erlach. The portal is ornamented with statues of Hercules by Matthias Bernhard Braun. Once containing a theatre, where Beethoven reputedly performed, the building now houses the city archives.

Heading south along Husova you soon come to a crossroads. Just before turning left (east) onto Karlova, continue a little further on Husova to nos 19–21; here, behind a Venetian-Renaissance façade, is the **Czech Museum of Fine Arts** (České muzeum výtvarných umění; tel: 222 220 218; Tue–Sun 10am–6pm; www.cmvu.cz; charge), which puts on exhibitions of contemporary Bohemian art.

After visiting the museum, you may wish to slake your thirst next door at **U Zlatého tygra** (The Golden Tiger), see ⑪①, before turning back to Karlova.

Karlova

The narrow and twisting Karlova (Charles Lane) has long been the main link between the Charles Bridge and the Old Town Square and is part of the Royal Way *(see margin, left)*. Follow its course east to reach Little Square (Malé náměstí) and the Old Town Square (Staroměstské náměstí).

OLD TOWN SQUARE

Old Town Hall

Entering Little Square, on your left is the **Old Town Hall** ❷ (Staroměstská radnice). Originally founded in 1338, the building was composed of a collection of medieval buildings, purchased one by one over the years with the proceeds of the city's tax on wine.

The first feature to strike you as you approach is the **Astronomical Clock** (Orloj), which dates from 1410 – although it was transformed into the contraption you see today by one

Master Hanuš in 1490. According to legend he was blinded after completing his work, so that he could not replicate it anywhere else. He got his revenge by climbing into the mechanism and disabling it. Documentary evidence suggests, however, that he continued to maintain the clock, unblinded, for many years, though the clock did not work properly until it was overhauled in 1570.

The performance of the upper part of the clock draws hordes of tourists at the striking of the hour from 8am to 8pm. Death rings the death knell and turns an hourglass upside down. The 12 Apostles proceed along the little windows that open before the chimes, and a cockerel flaps its wings and crows. The hour strikes. To the right of Death, a Turk wags his head. The two figures on the left are allegories of Greed and Vanity.

The face of the clock underneath preserves the medieval view of the course of the sun and moon through the zodiac, with Prague and the earth located at the centre of the universe. Beneath that is the calendar, with signs of the zodiac and scenes from country life, symbolising the 12 months of the year. The calendar is a replica of the work executed by Czech painter Josef Mánes in 1866 and now in the Prague City Museum.

Just near the clock is the **main visitor entrance** (tel: 724 508 584; Mon 11am–6pm, Tue–Sun 9am–6pm; charge). Tours take in the 15th-century council chamber, Petr Parléř's Gothic chapel (with a view of the interior workings of the clock), as well as the dungeons, which were used by the Czech resistance as its headquarters during the Prague uprising at the end of World War II. Separate tickets can be purchased for access to the stairs or lift up the **tower** (Mon 11am–8pm, Tue–Sun 9am–8pm; charge).

Outside again, on the other side of the building is a small park. This was once occupied by a Gothic-style wing of the town hall, which was blown up by the Nazis on the day before the Red Army entered the city at the end of World War II.

Hus Memorial

Elsewhere in the square, the imposing memorial in the middle honours the great Protestant reformer Jan Hus and was erected on the 500th anniversary – 6 July 1915 – of his being burnt at the stake. The work of Czech sculptor Ladislav Šaloun, it features Hussites and Protestants around the figure of Hus, together with a mother and child symbolising rebirth. Since its unveiling it has formed a symbol of resistance to foreign occupation, from the fall of the Habsburg empire to the invasion of the Warsaw Pact troops in 1968.

Above from far left: elevator and stairs inside the Old Town Hall; fisherman emblem on a house in the Old Town; carved wooden detail of a lion eating a man on the Old Town Hall; many of the buildings in this area have been impressively restored.

Little Square
Each of the fine houses lining Malá náměstí its own peculiar history. At no. 11, for example, Agostino of Florence established the first documented apothecary in the city in 1353, while at no. 3, the first Czech Bible was printed in 1488.

Food and Drink
① U ZLATÉHO TYGRA
Husova 17; tel: 222 221 111; 3–11pm daily; €
Perhaps the most famous hostelry in Prague, the Golden Tiger was where Václac Havel took Bill Clinton in 1994 to show him a real Czech pub. Unfortunately, since then it has put up its prices and gone for the tourist dollar. Even so, its cellars still provide ideal conditions for the storage of the Pilsner dispensed upstairs.

St Nicholas's Church

In the northwest corner of the square is the white Baroque **Church of St Nicholas** (Kostel sv. Mikuláše; tel: 224 190 994; daily Mar–Oct 9am–5pm, Nov–Feb 9am– 4pm; free), built to designs by Kilián Ignaz Dientzenhofer between 1732 and 1735. The church owes its unusual proportions to the fact that it was originally hemmed in by houses which stood in front, completely separating it from the square. The dark statues on the outside are by Antonín Braun, a nephew of Matthias Bernhard Braun. The sparse interior is somewhat disappointing, having suffered at the hands of Emperor Joseph II, who closed the monastery connected to the church and had the building used as a warehouse.

Kinský Palace

In the northeast corner of the square is the Rococo **Kinský Palace** (Palác Kinských), also designed by Kilián Ignaz Dientzenhofer. It was from here in February 1948 that Communist leader Klement Gottwald made the speech that heralded in the totalitarian regime. The building now houses the National Gallery's collection of **Landscape painting from the 17th to the 20th Century** (see p.31). The ground-floor bookshop once formed the premises of Franz Kafka's father's haberdashery shop. Franz himself attended school elsewhere in the building.

House at the Stone Bell

To the right of the palace, at no. 13, is the 14th-century Gothic **House at the**

Stone Bell (Dům u kamenného zvonu; (tel: 224 827 526; Tue–Sun 10am–6pm; www.citygalleryprague.cz; charge), which hosts temporary exhibitions put on by the Prague City Gallery. The two neighbouring houses are connected by an arcaded passage with ribbed vaulting. The house to the left is the former **Týn School**, originally a Gothic building, but rebuilt in the style of a Venetian Renaissance loggia. On the right is the early neo-Classical **House at the White Unicorn** (Dům u bílého jednorožce; tel: 222 313 909; daily 10am–8pm; charge), which provides another venue for art exhibitions.

Týn Church

Rising up behind is the **Church of Our Lady before Týn** ❸ (Kostel Matky Boží pod Týnem; tel: 222 322 801; open for mass and July–Aug Mon–Fri 9am–noon, 1–2pm; free). Built in 1365, the Týn Church is famous for its iconic towers. One of them is actually shorter and thinner than the other, which has led to their being nicknamed Adam and Eve. Until 1621 this was the main church of the Hussites. One of their leaders, George of Poděbrady (1458–71) had a gold chalice set into the gable niche between the church's two towers as a symbol of the Hussite faith. When the Jesuits took over after 1620 it was replaced by a statue of the Virgin, the chalice being melted down to make her crown, halo and sceptre.

To find the church's entrance, walk down the passageway through the arch second from the left of the Týn

Court Astronomer
Tycho Brahe (1546– 1601) had an eventful life. As a student, his nose was cut off in a duel; thereafter, he wore a gold prosthetic one. He then fell in love with a commoner, whom he never married, yet lived with, happily, for the rest of his life. Along with their eight children, their household included a clairvoyant dwarf, a jester and a tame elk, which eventually died by falling down the stairs after drinking too much beer. Brahe himself died after suffering a burst bladder after a boozy dinner at court. He had apparently been too polite to leave the table to relieve himself.

School's four arches. Inside, the Baroque interior was commissioned by the Jesuits. The paintings on the high altar and on the side altars are by Karel Škréta. Other remarkable works of art include the Gothic Madonna (north aisle), the Gothic pulpit and the oldest remaining font in Prague (1414).

To the right of the high altar is the red marble tombstone of the Danish astronomer Tycho Brahe (1546–1601), who worked at the court of Rudolf II. The inscription on the slab translates as 'Better to be than to seem to be' *(see margin right)*. Note also the window immediately to the right of the south portal; although now blocked off, it once enabled the occupants of the neighbouring house at Celetna 3 to peer into the church. One resident who enjoyed this privilege was Franz Kafka, who lived there from 1896 to 1907.

Týn Court

Now take the lane called Týnská around the back of the church. On your left on the corner is the Renaissance **House at the Golden Ring** (Dům u zlatého prstenu; tel: 224 827 022; Tue–Sun 10am–6pm; charge), a branch of the Prague City Gallery showing 20th-century Czech art. To the right is the entrance to the Týn Court, also known by its German name, Ungelt. Through the arch is a courtyard, the origins of which go back to the 11th century, when it offered protection to visiting foreign merchants. It is now a beautiful setting for some unusual shops (herbal toiletries, puppets, antique books) and cafés.

Exiting at the far end of Týn Court, you emerge onto Malá Štupartská. Opposite is the **Church of St James ❹** (Kostel sv. Jakuba; tel: 222 828 816; Mon–Sat 9.30am–noon, 2–4pm, Sun 2–4pm; free). Built by the Minorites during the reign of Charles IV, the church was renovated in the Baroque period. Note the reliefs on the main portal and the ceiling frescoes, the painting on the high altar by Václav Vavřinec Reiner and the extravagant tomb of Count Vratislav Mitrovic, the work of Johann Bernhard Fischer von Erlach and Ferdinand Brokoff.

A more gruesome feature is the 400-year-old decomposed arm hanging on the west wall, supposedly amputated from a thief who tried to steal the jewels from the altar, but who was stopped, legend has it, by the Madonna grabbing his offending arm. The almost theatrical quality of the interior provides a fine setting for the frequent organ concerts given on the uniquely toned instrument dating from 1705.

SOUTHERN STARÉ MĚSTO

Carolinum and Estates Theatre

Leaving the church, head south (left) down Malá Štupartská, turn right onto Štupartská, follow the road round to the end, turn left and cross over Celetná to find the narrow passage to Kamzíkova at no. 10. At the end of the lane, turn left and on your right is the Charles University or **Carolinum ❺** (Karolinum), centred around the Gothic Rotlev House at Železná 9.

Above from far left:
Art Nouveau maiden on a house in Staré Město; the Old Town Square's Astonomical Clock and Týn Church.

Above from left:
the Estates Theatre;
restaurant sign;
pretty back-street;
Bethlehem Chapel.

Founded by Charles IV in 1348, the university soon became associated with the Protestant reformers, and Jan Hus was rector here from 1402. Around the corner, on the south side, you can see the magnificent oriel window, which is part of the Chapel of SS Cosmas and Damian and the only true remnant of the original 14th-century Gothic building. Today, the complex is used for graduation ceremonies and is closed to the public.

Next door is the neo-Classical **Estates Theatre** (Stavovské divadlo; tel: 224 215 001; www.estatestheatre.cz; *see p.122*), which originally opened in 1783 as the Nostitz Theatre, named after Count Nostitz who paid for it. In its earlier history, it played largely to upper-class German audiences, hence its current name – the 'Estates' were the German nobility. Famously, this was where Mozart conducted the première of *Don Giovanni* in 1787. It was also the site, in 1834, of the first performance of the Czech national anthem, *Kde domov můj?* (Where is My Home?), originally part of the musical *Fidlovačka*.

Bethlehem Square

Now make your way down Havelská, just opposite the Carolinum. On your left is the 13th-century **Church of St Gall** (Kostel sv. Halva) with its onion domes (added in 1722), while on your right, down Melantrichova is a handy lunch option, see ⑪②.

At the end of Havelská you come out into Uhelný Trh, once the site of the town's coal market. On the far side of the square, continue down Skořepka, then turn right onto Husova. Soon afterwards is a turning on the left for **Bethlehem Square** (Betlémské náměstí).

Bethlehem Chapel

On the north side of the square, on your right, is the **Bethlehem Chapel** ❻ (Betlémská kaple; tel: 224 248 595; Apr–Oct Tue– Sun 10am–6.30pm,

---

Food and Drink

② COUNTRY LIFE
Melantrichova 15; tel: 224 213 373/366; Mon–Thur 9am–8.30pm, Fri 9am–3pm, Sun 11am–6pm; €
Run by the Seventh Day Adventists, this is haven for desperate vegetarians amongst all the butchery proffered everywhere else in Prague. Line up and take what you want from the salad bar and hot dishes (all food is organically grown). When you get to the checkout, your plate is weighed and the cost is calculated.

③ KLUB ARCHITEKTŮ
Betlémské náměstí 5a; tel: 224 401 214; daily 11.30am–midnight; €–€€
This place has a bookshop on the ground floor, a first-floor gallery and a restaurant in the cellars. The food is generally Mediterranean in style and very good value for money.

④ KRÁSNÝ ZTRÁTY
Náprstkova 10; tel: 775 755 143; Mon–Fri 10am–2am, Sat–Sun noon–2am; €
Stylish and informal café-cum-wine-bar-cum-gallery also hosting literary evenings and concerts. Breakfasts include bacon and cheese, and yoghurt and fruit. The rest of the day, choose from quesadillas, lasagne, sausages, salads, vegetarian dishes, honey cake and ice cream. After 11.30pm only pickled camembert-style cheese is served!

⑤ LE CORNICHON
Betlémská 9; tel: 222 211 766; Mon–Sat 4–11pm; €€€
Smart but not starchy restaurant with a modern and well-designed interior. The French-inspired menu is very fairly priced considering the quality of both ingredients and cooking. Start with snail casserole, *foie gras* or veal sweetbread ravioli. Follow with sea bass with ratatouille, duck with olives and turnips or hare à la royale. Finish with a selection of cheeses. Classic French wines are also sold in the associated shop.

Nov–Mar 10am–5.30pm; charge). It was here that Jan Hus delivered his fiery Reformationist sermons (in Czech rather than Latin) from 1402 until shortly before his martyrdom in 1415. A century later, in 1521, Thomas Münzer, the leader of the German peasants' revolt, also preached here.

The building dates from 1391. Its plain interior, which could hold up to 3,000 people, had the pulpit as its focal point rather than the altar. However, once Protestantism was banned in the 17th century, the building was taken over by the Jesuits, who converted it into a wood store. It was then demolished in 1786. Fortunately, it was meticulously reconstructed in its original form from 1950 to 1954, partly making use of original building materials. The Communist authorities seem to have viewed Hus as being an authentic working-class hero. Three of the original walls remain, and show heavily restored fragments of the scriptures painted on them to help parishioners follow the service. Hus's quarters are next door and accommodate an exhibition on his life and work.

On the east side of the chapel precinct is the design gallery, shop and restaurant, **Klub Architektů**, see ⑪③.

Ethnographic Museum

On the west side of Bethlehem Square is an archway leading to another courtyard. This gives access to the **Ethnographic Museum** ❼ (Náprstkovo muzeum; Tue–Sun 10am–6pm; www.aconet.cz/npm; charge). The museum is named after Vojta Náprstek (1826–

94). His fortune derived from brewing, and he chose to spend it on his two passions – ethnography and technology. His gadgets are now in the National Technical Museum (Národní technické muzeum; Kostelní 42; tel: 220 399 111; www.ntz.cz) in Holešovice *(see p.82–9)*, while his Asian, African and American collections are housed here, in the former brewery. He also established here the country's first women's club, whose meeting room has been preserved just as it was, complete with the hole Náprstek had drilled through the wall from his office.

The ground floor holds temporary exhibitions, while the first floor has the permanent collection of American Indian cultures. Among the exhibits are feathered Apache headdresses, beautiful papooses from California and fine Inuit garments. The galleries continue with the Central and South American holdings, featuring brightly coloured textiles and stylised Huaxtec figures.

On the second floor are Australian, Polynesian and Melanesian exhibits: Aboriginal paintings, boomerangs and harpoons, and a lovely model of a fish. Look out especially for the decorated skulls from the Solomon Islands and, of course, the large totem pole from Papua New Guinea. The museum's collection has also recently been augmented with private donations of two significant groups of African sculpture.

When you have finished, be sure to take advantge of the good options for drinks, snacks or more substantial meals, see ⑪④ and ⑪⑤, just around the corner from the museum.

Rotunda

To the south and parallel to Betlémská is Konviktská, where, at the end of the street, is the Rotunda of the Holy Cross (Rotunda sv. Kříže), a minute church built in the 12th century. It was supposedly built absolutely round, so that there were no sheltered corners for the devil to hide in.

Havel's Prison

The next street south again from Betlémská and Konviktská is Bartolomějská. During the Communist era, the former convent at no. 9 was used as a detention centre by the secret police (StB). Václav Havel was one of the many dissidents locked up and interrogated here. It has since been restored to the Grey Sisters, who now run it as a simple hotel (www.unitas.cz).

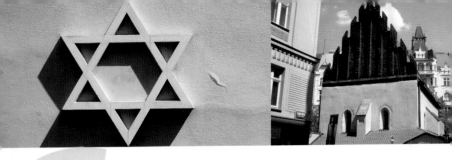

JOSEFOV

Walk in the footsteps of Franz Kafka around the cobbled streets of Josefov, the Jewish Quarter, visiting its historic synagogues and old cemetery, drinking up its café life, and immersing in its timeless stories and atmosphere.

DISTANCE 1.25km (1 mile)
TIME A half-day
START Little Square
END Spanish Synagogue
POINTS TO NOTE
The historic Jewish sites on this route are closed on Saturdays.

The first Jewish community in Prague was founded in 1091. Despite periods of oppression and laws restricting Jewish residents to only a small area of the city, the community flourished nevertheless, becoming a focal point for Jewish culture in Central Europe. Greater religious freedom finally came with the Age of Enlightenment and Emperor Joseph II's

Franz Kafka

Despite the fact that he wrote in German, Franz Kafka (1883–1924) is probably the Czech Republic's most famous author . His stories, with the notable exception of *The Metamorphosis* (1915), were only published after his early death from tuberculosis. His most famous works include *The Trial* (1925) and *The Castle* (1926), and concern troubled individuals in a nightmarishly impersonal and bureaucratic world.

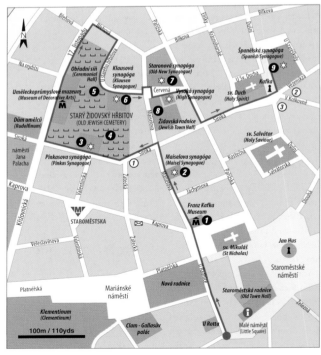

Patent of Toleration of 1781. The ghetto was later renamed Josephstown (Josefov) in his honour. Then in 1848 the old segregation laws were at last repealed and the Jewish community was allowed to develop freely.

One legacy of the centuries of discrimination, however, was that the quarter had never been provided with adequate sanitation. By the 1890s, the area was deemed a health hazard and almost all of it was demolished. Fortunately, the Jewish Town Hall, six synagogues and the Old Cemetery were all spared.

The community remained active until the Nazi occupation in 1939. Mass deportations began in 1941 and went on to wipe out 90 percent of the population. The Nazis intended to create a 'museum of the extinct Jewish race' here, but after the liberation it instead became the home of the largest collection of sacred Jewish artefacts in Europe. Today, Prague's Jewish community numbers around 7,000.

FRANZ KAFKA MUSEUM

The walk starts at the Little Square (Malé náměstí – near the Astronomical Clock at the western end of the Old Town Square). Turn right off the Little Square into U Radnice and then head north.

Very soon on your right at no. 5 is the block where the writer Franz Kafka was born in 1883 (see margin left). Little remains of the original fabric – only the stone portal – after a fire in 1887. Inside is the **Franz Kafka**

Museum ❶ (Expozice Franze Kafky; tel: 224 227 452; Tue–Fri 10am–6pm, Sat 10am–5pm; charge), featuring photographs and manuscript material relating to the writer. Unfortunately, though, the 'museum' is overly commercial and has little of substance to detain you long.

MAISEL SYNAGOGUE

Continue north as the street becomes Maiselova to find the **Maisel Synagogue** ❷ (Maiselova synagoga) on your right. This, along with the other main Jewish sites in Josefov (except the Old-New and Jerusalem synagogues) constitutes the Jewish Museum (tel: 221 711 511; www.jewishmuseum.cz; Sun–Fri: Apr–Oct 9am–6pm, Nov–Mar 9am–4.30pm; charge); a single ticket gains entrance to all the sites.

The Maisel Synagogue itself was founded in the 1590s by Mordecai Maisel, the wealthy mayor of the quarter, but was destroyed in 1689 when a fire gutted much of the district. The present building, its replacement, was only given its neo-Gothic appearance at the end of the 19th century. Inside is an exhibition of manuscripts, prints, textiles and liturgical silverware.

PINKAS SYNAGOGUE

At the crossroads with Široká, turn left for the **Pinkas Synagogue** ❸ (Pinkasova synagoga; part of the Jewish Museum; admission times as above), originally founded in 1479 by Rabbi Pinkas, who had fallen out with the

Above from far left: Star of David; Old-New Synagogue; Kafka's typewriter; decorative ceiling; Spanish Synagogue.

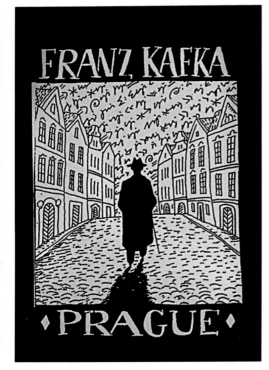

elders of the Old-New Synagogue. The present building, though, came into being in 1535, adapted from a house belonging to the prominent Horowitz family.

Since 1958 the synagogue has served as a memorial to 77,297 of the Czech Jewish victims of the Holocaust. The inscriptions around the interior walls list the name, date of birth and date of deportation of each victim. For many years these names were obscured – initially because of damp, then because the Communist authorities closed the synagogue, supposedly for

Below: front cover to a book on Kafka's Prague.

restoration, but actually neglecting it, seemingly out of antipathy to the Jewish cause after the Six Day War. In the 1990s, the names were carefully rewritten. A few remnants of the original wall can be seen.

Memorial

The synagogue now also serves as a memorial to the 7,500 children who died in Nazi concentration camps, and to the women who encouraged them to paint and draw while they were awaiting deportation from the holding camp at Terezín, in the Elbe Valley, approximately 60km (38 miles) to the north of Prague. The children's pictures, with their names and the dates of their death, line the walls of the first-floor gallery.

OLD JEWISH CEMETERY

The **Old Jewish Cemetery** ❹ (Starý židovský hřbitov; part of the Jewish Museum) is also accessed just nearby. It came into being in the 15th century, and burials continued here until 1787. The number of graves is much greater than the 12,000 gravestones would suggest – the true figure is probably closer to 100,000. Because this was the only place where Jews could be buried, graves were piled layer on layer.

The majority of the inscriptions on the stones are poetic texts of grief and mourning. The reliefs give the family name or emblem, and the profession of the deceased (scissors for a tailor, for example). The oldest monument in the cemetery is the tombstone of the poet Avigdor Kara, dating from 1439. Also

Above from far left: the Old Jewish Cemetery; Holocaust Memorial in the Pinkas Synagogue; Ceremonial Hall.

buried here, in 1601, was the noted Jewish mayor Mordecai Maisel. But the most famous tomb is that of the great scholar Rabbi Löw (1525–1609), who supposedly created the Golem *(see box below)*.

CEREMONIAL HALL

Back on Široká again, continue to the end of the street and then turn right onto 17 Listopadu. On your left, on the banks of the river, is the Rudolfinum while on your right is the Museum of Decorative Arts *(see p.60)*. Continue north, skirting the perimeter wall of the Jewish Cemetery, and turn right into Břehová and then right again into U starého hřbitova.

First on your right is the neo-Romanesque **Ceremonial Hall** ❺ (Obřandí šín; part of the Jewish Museum), built in 1911 for the Prague Burial Society, which performed charitable duties as well as burials. Inside is an exhibition devoted to Jewish life and traditions, with particular emphasis on medicine, illness and death within the ghetto.

KLAUSEN SYNAGOGUE

Next door is the **Klausen Synagogue** ❻ (Klausova synagoga; part of the Jewish Museum), a Baroque building with a long hall and barrel vaulting. It was built in 1694 to replace the little 'cells': three buildings that served as houses of prayer, classrooms and a ritual bath. It now houses an exhibition of Hebrew manuscripts, textiles and silver.

OLD-NEW SYNAGOGUE

Back outside, continue to the end of the road – where it meets Maiselova – and cross over to the **Old-New Synagogue** ❼ (Staronová synagóga; www. synagogue.cz; Sun–Thur 9.30am– 5pm, until 6pm Apr–Oct; charge). This synagogue is not part of the Jewish Museum, though the inexpensive admission fee also allows entry to the **Jerusalem Synagogue** (Apr–Oct Sun– Fri 1–5pm).

The Old-New Synagogue dates back to the 1270s, and is the oldest Jewish house of worship still in use in Europe. It was first called the New Synagogue, though gained its present name when another synagogue – now destroyed – was built close by. The building is an unparalleled example of a medieval two-aisled synagogue, with buttresses and a high saddle roof and brick gable (redolent of Cistercian Gothic).

The Golem

According to legend, Rabbi Löw created a 'Golem' to defend the Jewish Quarter after the emperor decreed that Prague's Jews were to be expelled or killed. The Rabbi made the Golem using clay from the banks of the Vltava, and brought it to life with mystical Hebrew incantations. As the Golem grew bigger, it became more violent and started killing gentiles. Before long, the emperor rescinded his decree and the Rabbi destroyed the Golem by rubbing out the first letter of the Hebrew word *emet* ('God's truth') from the Golem's forehead to leave the word *met* ('death'). Rabbi Löw stored the monster's remains in a coffin in the attic of the Old-New Synagogue so that it could be summoned again if needed.

The Interior

The interior is remarkably original, despite some 19th-century efforts at renovation. It had previously been left unaltered as a tribute to the 3,000 people who sought sanctuary here yet were slaughtered in the pogrom of 1389. In the vestibule are two early Baroque money boxes, used for collecting Jewish taxes from the entire kingdom. In the main aisle, between the two pillars, is the Almemor with its lectern for reading the Torah and sectioned off by a late-Gothic grille. In the middle of the east wall is the Torah shrine, called the Ark, with a triangular tympanum above. Next to the Ark is the Chief Rabbi's Chair, decorated with a Star of David. Among the other seats lining the walls is a tall one marked with a gold star. It belonged to Rabbi Löw.

Services in Hebrew are still held here on weekdays at 8am, Fridays at sundown and Saturdays at 9am. The only time in its history services have not been held was during the Nazi occupation.

JEWISH TOWN HALL

Opposite the Old-New Synagogue is the **Jewish Town Hall** ❹ (Židovská radnice). It was designed in 1586 in Renaissance style by Pankratius Roder for the mayor, Mordecai Maisel, although the newest, southern part dates only from the beginning of the 20th century. In keeping with the Hebrew practice of reading from right to left, the hands on the clock tower move in an anticlockwise direction.

High Synagogue

Originally part of the Jewish Town Hall, but in 1883 given a separate entrance, is the **High Synagogue** (Vysoká synagóga), opposite the Old-New Synagogue on Červená. It is no longer open for viewing.

SPANISH SYNAGOGUE

Now cut through Červená to emerge onto **Pařížká**, an Art Nouveau boulevard of shops and restaurants. Turn

---

Food and Drink

① KING SOLOMON

Široká 8; tel: 224 818 752; www.kosher.cz; Sun–Thur noon–11pm; €€€

The only strictly kosher restaurant in Prague. Hebrew-speaking staff. Among the classic dishes of Central European Jewish cooking are chicken soup, gefilte fish, carp with prunes, and duckling drumsticks with schollet and sautéed cabbage. Kosher wines are from Israel, Hungary, France and the Czech Republic. It is also possible to arrange Shabat meals beforehand and even have them delivered to your hotel (see their website for details).

② KOLKOVNA

V Kolkovně 8; tel: 224 819 701; daily 11am–midnight; €€

Though located in a former printing office in a fine 19th-century building, Kolkovna is a modern take on the traditional beer hall and is licensed from the Pilsner Urquell brewery. The décor is smart and understated (except for a slightly Captain Nemo copper-plated bar). The food is solid Czech fare – fried cheese, goulash, roast duck – and reasonably priced.

③ NOSTRESS

Dušní 10; tel: 222 317 004; Mon–Fri 8am–11pm, Sat–Sun 10am–11pm; €€€

Stylish café-restaurant with a gallery for contemporary photography attached. The daily lunch menus are reasonably priced (sandwiches and beer are also recommended). Dinner, however, is much more expensive. The well-executed cooking is generally of the fusion cuisine variety.

right, and when you meet Široká again, either turn right again for a good lunch destination, see ⑪①, or else turn left to continue the tour.

Continuing the walk eastwards, you soon encounter Jaroslav Rona's 2002 **Kafka Statue** on your left before reaching the **Spanish Synagogue** ❾ (Spanělská synagóga; part of the Jewish Museum). This restored Reform synagogue was built in 1868 on the site of an earlier place of worship (older even than the Old-New Synagogue). The synagogue takes its name from the Moorish-style stucco decoration of the interior – an imitation of the style widely used in parts of Spain, including the Alhambra. On the ground floor is an exhibition on Jewish life in the region from the 19th century onwards. The first floor holds a collection of synagogue silver from Bohemia and Moravia.

ENDING THE TOUR

On completing your Jewish cultural tour, take advantage of the area's excellent restaurants and bars: see ⑪② and ⑪③, just across the road.

Above from far left: puppets for sale in the Jewish Quarter; elaborate stonework on the side of the Spanish Synagogue.

Kafka's Haunts
Kafka lived as a child at U Minuty House at no. 2 in the Old Town Square (Staroměstské náměsti). He attended school at no. 12 (the Kinský Palace), where, in the same building, his father also had his haberdashery shop (now occupied by the Franz Kafka Bookstore). Later, at no. 5 (Oppelt House) he wrote most of *The Castle*, and then at no. 18, The House of the Unicorn, he frequented a literary salon. For worship, Kafka attended the Old-New Synagogue (where his bar mitzvah was held).

Left: the ornate Moorish interior of the Spanish Synagogue.

THE RUDOLFINUM TO THE CUBISM MUSEUM

This route skirts the edge of the Old Town and is a good guide to the different styles of Czech architecture and design, from the early Gothic in the Medieval Art Gallery to the Art Nouveau Municipal House.

DISTANCE 2km (1¼ miles)
TIME A full day
START The Rudolfinum
END The Powder Tower
POINTS TO NOTE

This tour is quite art heavy, and, after two galleries, visitors might be reluctant to see a third; however, continuing the route on the Cubist museum is highly recommended. If it is any incentive, the Grand Café Orient on the first floor is a good place to rest any aching feet.

Start this tour of the outskirts of the Old Town at náměstí Jana Palacha. Staroměstská metro station is close by, on Kaprova; from there, turn left out of the station and walk down towards to the river to enter the square.

THE RUDOLFINUM

Dominating the square is the **Rudolfinum** ❶ (www.rudolfinum.cz), an impressive neo-Renaissance building built as a concert hall from 1875 to 1884. From 1918 to 1938 it was the seat of the Czechoslovak Parliament, but after World War II it was returned to its original use as the home of the Czech Philharmonic Orchestra, who regularly perform in its magnificent Dvořák Hall. The Galerie Rudolfinum (www2. rudolfinum.org) is an important venue for the work of well-known, often foreign, artists and also has a lovely café.

MUSEUM OF DECORATIVE ARTS

Across the road – no.17. listopadu – from the Rudolfinum is the UPM or **Museum of Decorative Arts** ❷ (Uměleckoprůmyslové muzeum; tel: 251 093 111; www.upm.cz; Tue 10am–7pm, Wed–Sun 10am–6pm; charge). The building, itself a fine example of the decorative arts, was built between 1897 and 1900.

This is one of the best-displayed, and most interesting, museums in Prague. The exhibits are displayed by process and material: 'The Story of Fibre' (textiles and fashion); 'Born in Fire' (ceramics and glass); 'Treasury' (covering metals); and 'Print & Image' (graphic design and photography).

The Collections

Each section has some wonderful items, but among the best are the collections of

Rudolfinum Statues
When the Nazis occupied Prague they wanted to get rid of the statue of the German Jewish composer Mendelssohn from the Rudolfinum. Unfortunately for them, they removed the statue of the revered German composer Richard Wagner by mistake.

late-19th- and 20th-century women's costume. Among many fine pieces are an adventurous day dress in a hand-woven fabric (1926) by Marie Teinit-zerová, a 1930s sunbathing outfit of a bodice, shorts and sleeveless jacket, and two great 1960s Op Art-influenced swimsuits. The collections include not only clothing but an excellent selection of shoes and accessories.

The glass and ceramics collection includes some fine examples of 16th- to 17th-century Venetian glass, but, of course, it is the Bohemian work that is best represented. Particularly good are the four cases that show the develop-ment of faience, glass and ceramics from Art Nouveau, via Cubism, Art Deco and the 1950s, to the present day. Of the imaginatively displayed metalwork, it is probably those pieces of 1900–30 that are most interesting; look out for Josef Gočár's Cubist clock (1913). There are also fine examples of 20th-century jew-ellery, particularly those pieces from the 1970s and 1980s by Jozef Soukup.

The Czechs have long had a repu-tation for good graphic design, and this is borne out by the displays of early 20th-century posters; chief among these are those displaying the influence of Cubism. As well as a display of experimental photography from the *fin de siècle* to the 1940s, there is a case of drawers showing the changes in typographical design from the 15th to the 20th century.

CUBIST ARCHITECTURE AND LUNCH OPTIONS

Turn right out of the museum, along the wall of the Old Jewish Cemetery *(see p.56)* and then turn right into Břehová, which brings you out into an open square. On your left is **Les Moules**, see ⑪①, a good place for lunch. Cross over the wide street of Pařížská and take Bílkova, the road directly in front of you. As you leave the square look to your left along Elišky Krásnohorské and there is a **Cubist apartment block ❸** built by Otakar Novotný in 1919–21.

Continue to the end of the road and turn right, and at the next junction take the second left into Haštalská. Here you will find a second good option for a lunch stop, **Chez Marcel**, see ⑪②.

Above from far left: the Rudolfinum; stained glass at the Museum of the Decorative Arts; sphinx at the Rudolfinum; inside the Museum of the Decorative Arts.

Cubist Design
In the Museum of Decorative Arts look out for Pavel Janák's black-and-white Cubist ceramics. This iconic design is one of those that can be bought in the Kubista shop below the House of the Black Madonna *(see p.19)*.

Food and Drink

① LES MOULES
Pařížská 19; tel: 222 315 022; daily 9am–midnight; €€–€€€
Within sight of the Old-New Synagogue, this Belgian bar and restaurant is a good place to while away a few hours. As well as an excellent variety of Belgian beer, bottled and on tap, the food is both delicious and filling, with pride of place going to the mussels.

② CHEZ MARCEL
Haštalská 12; tel: 222 315 676; Mon–Fri 8am–1am, Sat–Sun 9am–1am; no credit cards; €€
Very French, even down to the occasionally grumpy service, and good value, this bistro opposite St Agnes's Convent has all the expected dishes (omelettes, steak and salads), plus French wines by the glass. Tasty, simple food of the sort that is typical in France.

Above from left:
Municipal House;
House of the Black
Madonna; Powder
Tower; resurrected
Christ from the
Třeboň altarpiece,
St Agnes's Convent.

ST AGNES'S CONVENT

In front of the restuarant is the church of St Hastala, and behind this – take the lane to the right of the church – is **St Agnes's Convent** ❹ (Anežský klášter; U milosrdných 17). The convent is the first early-Gothic building in Prague, having been founded in 1234. However, the complex fell into decay and parts of it were completely destroyed. After many years, restorers succeeded in bringing some rooms back to their original state. These were linked to form the present-day historic complex by means of carefully reconstructed additions.

The convent buildings hold the National Gallery's collection of **Medieval Art in Bohemia and Central Europe** (Středověké umění v Čechách; tel: 224 810 628; www.ngprague.cz; Tue–Sun 10am–6pm; charge). The superb collection has been sensitively displayed and fits well into the space.

The Collections

The exhibits are shown in broadly chronological order, starting with a very important early wooden statue, the *Madonna of Strakonice* (c.1300–20). Among the star exhibits are the museum's two Bohemian altarpieces: the first from Vyšší Brod (1350) and the second from Třeboň (1380–5), whose artist was one of the most important figures of the International Style. Also look out for the series from the Chapel of the Holy Cross at Karlštejn (1360–4) by Master Theodoric.

Later works are displayed in the long final gallery. Influence from the Netherlands can be seen in Hans Pleydenwurff's *Beheading of St Barbara* (c.1470), and, at the end of the 15th century, from the Italian Renaissance in the work of the Master of Grossgmain. As well as some fabulous Swabian and Bohemian woodcarving, there are two excellent paintings by Lucas Cranach the Elder (the *Madonna of Poleň*, 1520, and *Young*

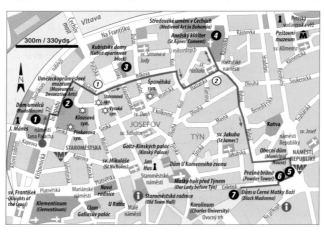

Lady with a Hat, 1538). The galleries end with a display of woodcuts, notably Dürer's *Apocalypse* (1511) and *The Passion Cycle* (1509) by Cranach.

MUNICIPAL HOUSE

Now return to Haštalská and at the end of the street turn right into Rybná. Walk down Rybná, past the Modernist Hotel Josef designed by Eva Jiřičná, to the Hotel Paříž. The short streets of Obecního domu bring you out into náměstí Republiky (Republic Square). Here is the splendid Art Nouveau **Municipal House ❺** (Obecní dům; tel: 222 002 101; www.obecni-dum.cz; daily 10am– 7pm; tours in both Czech and English).

History

Built from 1906 to 1911, it was created in response to the politically and economically strengthened national consciousness of the Czech bourgeoisie around the turn of the 20th century. A whole generation of artists worked on this building, including Alfons Mucha (1860–1939), who has left here some wonderful examples of his art. Every corner of the building, both inside and out, is elegantly decorated, and has been carefully maintained over the years. It was also here that the independent Czechoslovak Republic was declared in October 1918.

Current Use

Today, the building is home to the Prague Symphony Orchestra (www.fok.cz), which plays in the ornate Smetana Hall (Smetanova síň). Some idea of the splendour of the building can be gained from its café and restaurants.

POWDER TOWER

Adjoining the Municipal House, on Celetná, is the late-Gothic **Powder Tower ❻** (Prašná brána; daily Apr– Oct 10am–6pm; charge). It was built in the second half of the 15th century as a city gate and acquired its name when it was used as a gunpowder storehouse; the neo-Gothic roof was added during the 19th century. It is now used for temporary exhibitions.

CUBISM MUSEUM

Walking down Celetná will bring you to the the Cubist **House of the Black Madonna ❼** (Dům u Černé Matky Boži), home to the **Museum of Czech Cubism** (Ovocný trh 19; tel: 224 211 746l; www.ngprague.cz; Tue–Sun 10am–6pm; charge). The entrance to the museum is via a beautiful spiralling staircase with a Cubist motif on the bannister supports. The permanent galleries are on the second, third and fourth floors. Here there are works by Czech doyens of the movement, including Otto Gutfreund (1889–1927), Pavel Janák (1882–1956), Emil Filla (1882–1953), Josef Gočár (1880–1945), Jaroslav Benda (1882–1970) and Bohumil Kubišta (1884–1918). There are paintings, sculpture, furniture and graphic design, but the star exhibit is probably the building itself, as beautifully designed inside as out.

Sharp Design
Although it is hard to see from walking around the outside of the building, the layout of the Municipal House (Obecní dům) is very clever. Laid out on a triangular site, the almost symmetrical building is in the shape of an arrow head, with the concert hall neatly placed at its centre.

WENCESLAS SQUARE

With its Art Nouveau buildings and historic monuments, Wenceslas Square has witnessed the proclamation of independence in 1918, the Prague Spring in 1968 and the Velvet Revolution in 1989.

Above: Art Nouveau hotel sign; memorial to one of the students who burnt themselves alive in protest against the Communist Regime, Wenceslas Square.

DISTANCE 2.5km (1½ miles)

TIME 2 hours

START National Museum

END Můstek metro station

POINTS TO NOTE

The nearest metro station to this route's starting point is Muzeum, at the intersection of lines A and C.

Wenceslas Square (Václavské náměstí) is actually more of a broad boulevard than an open square. Sloping down for almost half a mile at the heart of Nové Město (New Town), its wide pedestrian zones follow the course of the fortifications that surrounded the city in the Middle Ages, before Charles IV erected the New Town in a semicircle around the old.

History of the Square

Although the square was originally used as a horse market, it eventually became the setting for much grander events. All Prague's historic uprisings – from the Reformationist Hussite Rebellion in the early 15th century to the nationalist riots in 1848 to the remarkably peaceful Velvet Revolution in 1989 – have focused on the square.

In the last century, crowds assembled here for the proclamation of independence for Czechoslovakia in 1918. Then in March 1939, the Nazis took away that independence and celebrated their bloodless conquest with a military parade here. In 1968, Soviet tanks rolled into the square to crush the Prague Spring and with it, Alexander Dubček's aspirations for 'socialism with a human face'. Finally, in 1989 the square was the

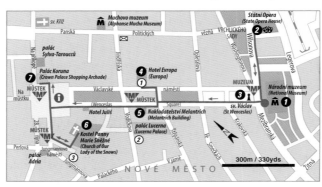

rallying point for the series of demonstrations that led to the Velvet Revolution and the country's independence.

The Square Today

Since those heady days, however, the square has lost some of its lustre. Burger bars, casinos, strip clubs, souvenir stalls and parked cars now set the tone, though the city authorities are slowly waking up to the need for renewal. A competition has led to the appointment of architect Jakub Cigler to restore the square's fortunes. The National Museum will be reintegrated with the square, green spaces will be reinstated, cars re-routed to a new city ring road. Questions remain, however, regarding funding, and it is unclear when the plans will come to fruition.

NATIONAL MUSEUM

The route begins at the southern end of the square, at the **National Museum** ❶ (Národní muzeum; tel: 224 497 111; www.nm.cz; daily: May–Sept 10am–6pm, Oct–Apr 9am–5pm, closed first Tue in the month; charge). Constructed between 1885 and 1890 to designs by Josef Schulz, this neo-Renaissance palace houses collections of natural and national history, as well as a large library. It is worth a quick visit, not so much for the exhibitions – which are used mainly to bore parties of schoolchildren – but for the lavish design of the grand entrance foyer, dignified with busts of famous Czechs.

In front of the museum, look out for two small mounds in the cobbled pavement. These mark the place where a Czech student named Jan Palach set himself on fire in January 1969 in protest against Soviet oppression. A month later, another student, Jan Zajíc, did the same.

STOCK EXCHANGE BUILDING

Just to the east of the National Museum, along Wilsonova (named after President Wilson, who, after World War I, championed the principle of self-determination that led to

Above from far left: the illuminated National Museum; interior of the National Museum; Wenceslas Square.

Wenceslas

While famous elsewhere as the 'Good King Wenceslas' of the Christmas carol, to the Czechs Wenceslas was not a king at all, but the Duke of Bohemia and their country's patron saint. He lived c.907–35 and was brought up as a Christian by his grandmother, St Ludmila, before taking the reins of state, founding the Church of St Vitus (now the cathedral) and then being murdered on the orders of his younger brother while on his way to church. His feast day is 28 September, and, since the year 2000, this day has been celebrated as a national holiday.

Above from left:
ballet at the State Opera; the lush auditorium; portal on Na Příkopě *(see p.69)*; Grand Hotel Europe.

the independence of Czechoslovakia) is the old **Stock Exchange building**. This was transformed into a glass structure to house the Federal Assembly between 1966 and 1972. It now houses Radio Free Europe, broadcasting US propaganda to Muslim Fundamentalist audiences, and, as such, requires concrete barriers and armed guards.

STATE OPERA HOUSE

Just beyond it is the **State Opera House ❷** (Státní Opera; www.opera. cz; *see p.122*), built in 1888 and renowned for having one of the most beautiful auditoriums in Central Europe. Among the famous conductors and singers to have worked here are Gustav Mahler, Richard Strauss, Nellie Melba and Benjamino Gigli. The theatre's reputation was greatly enhanced under the stewardships of Alexander Zemlinksy (1911–27) and Georg Szell (1927–38), who staged works by their contemporaries, Krenek,

Hindemith and Schreker. Nowadays, it puts on an annual festival of Italian opera in August and September.

Beyond the opera house is the city's **main railway station** (Hlavní nádraží), with its Art Nouveau structure and Communist-era additions.

STATUE OF ST WENCESLAS

Back on Wenceslas Square, in front of the National Museum, with a commanding position, is the equestrian **Statue of St Wenceslas ❸** by Josef Myslbek, erected in 1912 after 30 years of planning and design. The base, designed by Alois Dryák, depicts saints Agnes, Adelbert, Procopius and Ludmila (Wenceslas's grandmother). It was from here that Alois Jirásek read the proclamation of Czechoslovakian independence to the assembled crowds on 28 October 1918. A less happy event, though, is memorialised a little way down from the statue, in the form of a headstone featuring the images of Palach and Zajíc.

ART NOUVEAU ARCHITECTURE

Continue the walk along the right-hand side of the square. You will soon catch the seductive whiff of frying sausages from the square's many sausage kiosks. If, however, your taste is for something more refined, you will soon arrive at the magnificent **Hotel Evropa ❹**, at nos 25–7. This grand Art Nouveau establishment is the result of architect Alois Dryák's

---

Food and Drink 🍴

① KAVÁRNA EVROPA
Václavské náměstí 25; tel: 224 228 117; 9.30am–11pm; €€
The magnificent Art Nouveau interior of this café gives a taste of old-world style. The food, however, is decidedly mediocre and overpriced, so stay only so long as to take in the atmosphere.

② KAVÁRNA ŘEHOŘ SAMSY
Vodičkova 30 (pasáž U Nováků); tel: 224 225 413; 9.30am–7pm; €
This bookshop-cum-café takes its name from the protagonist of Franz Kafka's *Metamorphosis*. Tucked away in one of the passages off the Lucerna shopping arcade, it is a welcome haven from the brash commercialism of Wenceslas Square. As well as excellent coffee, the café serves light snacks, wines and beers (including very good Polička). Friendly service.

makeover of the building in 1905 (with the assistance of architectural sculptor Ladislav Šaloun). Make a pit-stop at the stylish café, see ⑪①, and before moving on, have a shufti at the hotel's atrium and other public rooms (used in the film *Mission Impossible*).

Melantrich Building

Next, cross over to the other side of the square and the **Melantrich Building** ❺ (Nakladatelství Melantrich; built 1914) at no. 36. It was on the balcony here on 24 November 1989 that Alexander Dubček and Václav Havel appeared together before a crowd of 300,000 people in a pivotal event of the Velvet Revolution. The building is now occupied by Marks & Spencer.

Just nearby, at no. 34, is the Wiehl House, built in 1896 to designs by Antonín Wiehl. Its extravagant façade is decorated with neo-Renaissance murals by Czech artist Mikuláš Aleš and others.

Lucerna Palace Shopping Arcade

Tucked away behind, in the block between Štěpánská and Vodičkova, is the labyrinthine **Lucerna Palace** (Palác Lucerna) shopping arcade. This Art Nouveau complex harbours the gorgeous **Lucerna cinema** (operating since 1909) and associated bar (now somewhat louche, though it retains its stylish décor), as well as a grand con-cert hall and several cafés – including the book café, **Řehoř Samsa**, see ⑪②.

Below: upside-down statue of Wenceslas and his horse, in the Lucerna Shopping Arcade.

Mucha Museum

The life and work of the Czech Art Nouveau artist Alphons Mucha (1860–1939) are showcased at the Mucha Museum (Muchovo muzeum; Panská 7; tel: 221 451 333; www.mucha.cz; daily 10am–6pm; charge), on Panská, northeast of and parallel to Wenceslas Square. The collection includes around 100 exhibits including paintings, photographs, charcoal drawings, pastels, lithographs and personal memorabilia. Mucha is probably Bohemia's most famous exponent of the Art Nouveau style; he is chiefly known for his work in Paris, where he lived from 1887 to 1904.

Hanging from the ceiling of the atrium by the cinema is David Černy's amusing sculpture of King Wenceslas on his upside-down horse, a satire on the monumental version in the square outside.

MODERNIST ARCHITECTURE

Out in the fresh air again, continue your walk down the square, passing Ludvík Kysela's **Alfa Palace** at no. 28 and Pavel Janák's **Hotel Juliš** at no. 22 – both 1920s Modernist affairs. At no. 12 is a brief Art Nouveau diversion, the **Peterka House**, built to Jan Kotěra's designs in 1899–1900, while close by, at no. 8, is Blecha and Králíček's **Adam Pharmacy** (built 1911–13). At no. 6 is the 1929 Functionalist building designed by Ludvík Kysela for Tomáš Bat'a, art patron, progressive industrialist and founder of the shoe empire.

OUR LADY OF THE SNOWS

When you come to Kysela's Lindt Building at no. 4, turn left into the passageway through the middle to emerge on the other side in Jungmannovo náměstí. Look out for the memorial to Josef Jungmann (1773–1847), who revived the Czech language. On your left, outside the gate of the Franciscan rectory, is a **Cubist lamppost**, designed by Emil Králíček in 1913. Behind this is the **Church of Our Lady of the Snows** ❻ (Kostel Panny Marie Sněžné; tel: 222 246 243; daily 9am–5.30pm; free), which can be accessed via a gateway around the corner.

History

Completed in 1347, the church was planned as a coronation church by Charles IV. The designs envisaged a three-aisled Gothic cathedral church and the tallest building in Prague. However, shortage of money and the start of the Hussite Wars meant the plans were never fulfilled. In fact, it was from here that the radical Hussites marched to the New Town Hall in 1419 in order to teach the city's officials a lesson, in one of Prague's infamous defenestrations (see p.22).

Food and Drink

③ LAHŮDKYZLATÝ KŘÍŽ

Jungmannova 34; tel: 221 191 801; Mon–Fri 6.30am–7pm, Sat 9am–3pm; €

Don't get ripped off at the tourist restaurants on Wenceslas Square. Instead, follow the stream of ordinary Czechs a few paces from the square to this nondescript shop on a side street. Inside, behold a delicatessen classic. Jolly, motherly types serve you from behind refrigerated counters rammed full of typical Czech snack food – *chlebíčky*. A slice of white bread is loaded up with ham or salami or maybe smoked salmon, with a dollop or two of cream cheese or potato salad on top, and maybe a gherkin garnish or a little caviar. Order a side of coleslaw or aubergine salad. And take advantage of the beer on tap. Then eat and drink standing up at one of the metal counters, or repair to the garden around the corner. And all very cheap indeed.

The Interior

Today, all that can be seen of Charles IV's grand plan is the out-of-proportion chancel with its extravagant black-and-gold Baroque altarpiece. The painting on the altar (by an unknown Italian artist) depicts the legend of Our Lady of the Snows. In the 4th century AD, the Virgin Mary appeared in a Roman merchant's dream and told him to build a temple on the place where snow would be found the following morning. When he woke up the next morning, the merchant was confused, since it was the middle of summer. Even so, he went out and he found that the Esquiline hill was covered in snow. Following the request, he had the Church of St Maria Maggiore built on the site.

If you are ready for lunch at this point, a fine Czech delicatessen just round the corner on Jungmannova should fulfil your requirements, see ⑪③.

SHOPPING

After lunch, retrace your steps to Wenceslas Square, cross over, and at the other corner you will find the monumental **Crown Palace Shopping Arcade** ❼ (Palác Koruna). Built between 1912 and 1914 to designs by Antonín Pfeiffer and Matěj Blecha, it shows early hints of Modernism.

Outside again, the street that runs perpendicular to Wenceslas Square is Na Příkopě (or 'On the Moat'); it was originally built on top of a river (filled in in 1760) that separated the walls of Staré Město and Nové Město. Now an upmarket shopping street, it follows the line of the old fortifications all the way down to the Gothic Powder Tower at náměstí Republiky *(see p.63).*

This walk, however, ends here. And if you wish to catch the metro, take the escalators down to Můstek Station, at the intersection of lines A and B. 'Můstek' means 'little bridge', and as you descend you will see illuminated the stone remains of what was once a bridge that connected the fortifications of Prague's Old and New Towns. When workers were building the station a few decades ago, they had to be inoculated against the tuberculosis bacteria uncovered by their excavations. The bacteria had lain here dormant, encased in horse manure, since the Middle Ages.

Above from far left: Our Lady of the Snows; Koruna Shopping Arcade; wonderful Art Deco architectural details.

Below: tram near Wenceslas Square.

NOVÉ MĚSTO

This walk explores the artistic legacy of the Czech nationalist struggle through Prague's National Theatre and one of its greatest composers, Antonín Dvořák, as well as some interesting modern architecture.

DISTANCE 2.5km (1½ miles)
TIME A half-day
START National Theatre
END Dvořák Museum
POINTS TO NOTE
A varied walk that takes you from the river bank into the heart of the New Town's university district.

Goethe Institute
Masarykovo nábřeží.
on the western
(riverside) edge of
Nové Město, is lined
with elegant *fin-de-siècle* apartment
blocks. On the corner
of Na struze, which
runs southeast off
Masarykovo nábřeží,
is the Goethe
Institute, easily
recognisable by
the large eagle on
its façade. This was
the East German
Embassy during the
Cold War, but on
Reunification all
services moved to
the Lobkowicz Palace
in Malá Strana.

Prague's 'New Town' has a very different feel to the narrow streets of Staré Město (Old Town; *see p.46*) or Malá Strana (Lesser Town; *see p.38*). The grand 19th-century buildings conceal little gems, such as a Functionalist building for an artists' association, Gothic cloisters and a lovely botanical garden.

NATIONAL THEATRE

Begin your walk at the **National Theatre ❶** (Národní divadlo; *see p.122*), a fine reminder of the nation's enthu-siasm for culture in the late 19th century. In 1845 the Estates, with their German majority, turned down the request for a Czech theatre. In response, money was collected on a voluntary basis, and the building of a Czech theatre declared a national duty. In 1852 the site was bought, and the foundation stone was laid in 1868.

The building was designed by Josef Zítek in a style reminiscent of the Italian Renaissance. The theatre was completed by 1881 but then destroyed in a fire just before it was due to open. Undeterred, Czechs of all classes from all over the country once more contributed their coins to the rebuilding fund, and within nine months reconstruction could begin. Under Josef Schulz's direction, using many notable artists including Vojtěch Hynais, it was completed and opened in 1883 with a performance of Smetana's *Libuše*.

MODERNIST ARCHITECTURE

Head upstream along the river on Masarykovo nábřeží. On your right you will pass the wooded **Slavic Island ❷** (Slovanský ostrov), home to the Žofín concert hall (www.zofin.cz), where famous composers such as Berlioz, Liszt and Wagner have con-

Food and Drink
① LA PERLE DE PRAGUE
Rašínovo nábřeží; tel: 221 984 160; Mon 7–10.30pm, Tue–Sat noon–2pm, 7–10.30pm; €€€
A formal restaurant on top of the Tančící dům ('Fred and Ginger' building), with a menu of French and international dishes. The food is good, but the real attraction is the fabulous view over the city and river.

ducted. It is now a conference and cultural centre. At the far end of the island is the **Mánes House** (www.nadace-cfu.cz), an excellent example of Functionalist architecture. It was designed by Otakar Novotný from 1927 to 1930 for the Mánes Artists Association and now houses temporary exhibitions.

'Fred and Ginger' Building

Masarykovo nábřeží takes you to the Jirásek Bridge (Jiráskův most). Opposite the bridge, on the corner of Resslova, is Frank Gehry and Vlado Miluníc's Nationale Nederlanden Administrative Building, or **Tančící dům** ❸. Also nicknamed the 'Fred and Ginger' building on account of its supposed likeness to a dancing couple, it was built in 1992–6, and, now the novelty has worn off its faults have become apparent; it isn't well finished and the quirky design now seems like Postmodern grandstanding. However, it does have a pleasant small bar and café on the ground floor, and its rooftop restaurant, **La Perle de Prague** , see ⑪①, has wonderful views over the city.

NATIONAL MEMORIAL

Walk up Resslova and on your left you will come to the Orthodox Church of

Above from far left:
the dancing 'Fred and Ginger' building; Café Slavia (see p.117); National Theatre.

Resistance Heroes
On 17 May 1942 two parachutists sent from Britain by the Czechoslovak Government in exile succeeded in assassinating Reinhard Heydrich, the brutal Nazi governor (Reichsprotektor) of Bohemia and Moravia. After the murder, the assassins and five other members of the resistance movement barricaded themselves into the crypt of SS Cyril and Methodius. Their hiding place was discovered on 18 June, and they shot themselves rather than surrender to the SS. The Nazis exacted cruel revenge for the assassination: on 10 June 1942 his successor ordered the village of Lidice, some 25km (16 miles) from Prague, to be burnt to the ground. All the men in the village were shot and the women deported to concentration camps where many perished.

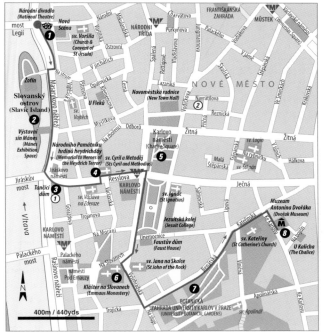

SS Cyril and Methodius (Kostel sv. Cyrila a Metoděje). The church is usually closed, but you can see through the windows in the porch into the ornate Baroque interior. Below, in the crypt is the **National Memorial to the Heroes of the Heydrich Terror** ➍ (Národního památníku hrdinů heydrichády; tel: 224 916 100; www.pravoslavnacirkev.cz; Apr–Sept: Tue–Sun 10am–5pm, Oct–Mar: Tue–Sun 10am–4pm; charge). A number of photographs, documents and a plaque are on display telling the story of the seven men who held out here after the assassination of Reichsprotektor Richard Heydrich *(see box below)*.

CHARLES SQUARE

At the top of Resslova is **Charles Square** ➎ (Karlovo náměstí), which was laid out during the construction of the New Town and which was once the site of the cattle market.

Faust House

On the right, south of some well-tended gardens, is the **Faust House**. According to legend, this was once the residence of the German magician and alchemist Dr Faustus, famed for selling his soul to the devil in exchange for power and knowledge, but was in fact the home of the English adventurer Edward Kelly, who promised Emperor Rudolf II a precious lump of gold from his alchemical laboratory. This he singularly failed to do and ended his life in one of the king's dungeons.

If you still have not eaten then try **Posezení u čiřiny**, see ⑪②, which is on Navrátilova off Vodičkova at the top left-hand corner of the square.

EMMAUS MONASTERY

To continue on your way, take Vyšehradská, south of the square to reach the **Emmaus Monastery** ➏ (Klášter na Slovanech; tel: 224 917 662; www.emauzy.cz; Mon–Fri 9am–5pm, Sat 11am–5pm; charge). Due to a location that controls access to the Vltava River, it has played a significant

Below: Art Nouveau decoration in Nové Město.

role in the city since it was founded by Charles IV in 1347.

A misconceived American bombing raid during World War II – the hapless pilots thought they were over Dresden, although that is no excuse – destroyed many of the monastery's irreplaceable medieval art treasures, but the magnificent cloisters alone make the place well worth a visit. The original Gothic towers were destroyed in the attack but replaced between 1965 and 1968 by the distinctive, overlapping concrete curves, topped with 1.3kg (nearly 3lbs) of gold. The two sail-shaped buttresses are considered to be one of the city's most striking pieces of modern architecture.

BOTANICAL GARDENS

At the bottom of Vyšehradská, past the Baroque Church of St John on the Rock, is the entrance to the **University Botanical Gardens** ❼ (Botanicka Zahrady University Karlovy v Praze; daily: Jan–Mar 10am–5pm, Mar–Oct 10am–6pm, Nov–Dec 10am–4pm; charge for the glasshouse). First set out in 1897, the gardens are one of the few stretches of greenery in the area. They are delightful; all the specimens are well labelled and the gardens are dotted with modern sculptures. The winding paths, rockeries and pools mean there are lots of quiet nooks and crannies to explore. The highlight is a beautiful series of restored pre-war greenhouses, dripping with tropical vegetation and including a delicious lily pond.

DVOŘÁK MUSEUM

After leaving the gardens take Benátská, the road leading up the hill past a number of university buildings. At the top take Kateřinská and turn right into Ke Karlovu. Here is the Villa Amerika, now housing the **Dvořák Museum** ❽ (Muzeum Antonína Dvořáka; tel: 224 918 013; www.nm.cz; Tue–Sun: Apr–Sept 10am–1.30pm, 2–5.30pm, Oct–Mar 9.30am–1.30pm, 2–5pm; charge), dedicated to one of the greatest Czech composers (1841–1904). This delightful little building, named after a 19th-century inn and designed by Kilián Ignaz Dientzenhofer, was built between 1717 and 1720 as a summer palace for the Michna family.

The Collection

The museum contains various Dvořák memorabilia, including his Bösendorfer piano and his viola, as well as displays of photographs and facsimiles of letters, tickets and manuscripts. On the first floor is a beautifully decorated little concert hall, where recitals are sometimes given. Although the labelling is in Czech, a guide in English can be borrowed from the front desk.

Michna Family
The Michnas of Vacínov were an important noble family in Bohemia during Habsburg times. As Catholics, they rose to prominence after the Hussite defeat at the Battle of the White Mountain in 1620. At one time they owned the huge castle of Konopiště and as well as employing Kilían Ignaz Dientzenhofer they also commissioned buildings from the Italian architect Carlo Lurago.

Food and Drink 🍴

② **POSEZENÍ U ČIRINY**
Navrátilova 6; tel: 222 231 709; Mon–Sat 11am–11pm; €€
A small but very good Czech and Slovak restaurant, tucked out of the way close to Charles Square. The menu covers a good range of traditional dishes, including *palačinky* (pancakes), roast pork and beef with a variety of sauces. Booking advised.

VYŠEHRAD

In legend this is where it all started: Vyšehrad was the rock on which Libuše and Přemysl founded the city. Today it is a site of nationalist pride and a burial ground for many famous Czechs.

DISTANCE 1km (½ mile)
TIME A half-day
START Vyšehrad metro station
END Vila Kovařovič
POINTS TO NOTE

While it is easiest to take the metro to the starting point, it is also possible to take a pleasant walk along the embankment of the River Vltava to reach Vyšehrad. Continue on from the Jirásek Bridge on route 9, and you will reach Vyšehrad in about 10 minutes.

Above: at Vyšehrad Cemetery; the view down to the Cubist Triple House and the River Vltava.

Vyšehrad is a rocky hill that rises from the place where the Vltava reaches the old city limits. According to legend it was here, in her father's castle, that Princess Libuše had her vision of the golden city of Prague: 'I see a great city, whose fame will reach to the stars... there in the woods you shall build your castle and your settlement, which shall

be named Praha.' Archaeologists doubt the veracity of this tale – Prague Castle was built in the 9th century; Vyšehrad was erected in the 10th century. But in the second half of the 19th century, at the peak of the Czech national revival, the story was irresistible to the likes of Smetana and Mendelssohn, and it formed the basis of their operas *Libuše* and *Libussa's Prophecy*.

Vyšehrad (literally 'high castle') has played a key role in Prague's history since the Přemyslid kings established it as their seat of power. Its tumultuous career as a battle fortress began in 1004, when it repelled the invading forces of Poland's Boleslav the Brave. Over the years the royal residence alternated between Vyšehrad and Hradčany, and the hill was repeatedly ransacked by foreign armies. Today, by contrast, the monuments of Vyšehrad are set in attractive parkland.

TÁBOR GATE

Begin the walk at **Vyšehrad metro station ❶** and take the steps that lead towards the imposing Communist-built Congress Centre (Kongresové-Centrum), formerly known as the Palace of Culture. Walk in front of the centre and descend the short flight of stairs onto Na Bučance and follow the signposts that

Food and Drink
① CAFFÉ FRESCO
Lumirova 33; tel: 234 724 230; daily 9am–10.30pm; €–€€
A pleasant modern café attached to a new hotel serving light Italian dishes, particularly good for a late breakfast or brunch on your way to the site. Tasty fresh pasta and salads are the mainstays of the menu and, as befits an Italian-inspired outfit, the coffee is excellent.

lead towards Vyšehrad. Carry straight on past **Caffé Fresco**, see ⑪①, a good place to refresh yourself before the sight-seeing ahead, below the 14th-century ramparts and turn right into the **Tábor Gate** ❷ (Táborská brána).

Just beyond the gate is the **Information Centre of the Vyšehrad National Cultural Monument** (Vyšehrad Národní Kulturní Památka; tel: 261 225 304; www.praha-vysehrad. cz; daily: Apr–Oct 9.30am–6pm, Nov–Mar 9.30am–5pm; charge for exhibitions on the site) housed in the remains of the Špička Gate.

ST MARTIN'S ROTUNDA

Ahead is the 17th-century Leopold Gate and, to the right, **St Martin's Rotunda** ❸ (Rotunda sv. Martina); open only for mass). This is a tiny Romanesque church dating from the 11th century, sensitively restored in the 1870s, and one of the oldest churches in the country, alongside St George's Basilica in Hradčany (see p.28).

DEVIL'S PILLAR

From here, take a left onto K Rotunde, with its low stone walls. Along this quiet street you'll pass on your right a lawn, where three short stone columns lean against each other at odd angles. This is the **Devil's Pillar**. It is said that a priest bet the devil that he could say mass before the devil could deliver a column from St Peter's Basilica in Rome. The devil took a column from a closer church, but St Peter intervened, waylaying the devil and breaking the pillar in three.

VYŠEHRAD PARK

Further on is the well-tended **Vyšehrad Park** and the **Church of SS Peter and Paul** ❹ (Kostel sv. Petra a Pavla; tel: 224 911 353; Wed–Sun 9am–noon, 1–5pm; charge), whose interior features Art Nouveau paintings of the saints. There has been a church here since the 11th century, but the present twin-spired neo-Gothic church dates to 1885.

Above from far left: portal on the Church of SS Peter and Paul; St Martin's Rotunda; statues and graves at the cemetery.

Holy Site There has been a place of worship on the site of the Church of SS Peter and Paul since the 11th century. The original church, which burnt down in the 13th century, was an important pilgrimage site as it contained relics of St Longinus, the soldier who pierced the side of Christ with a spear while he was suffering on the cross.

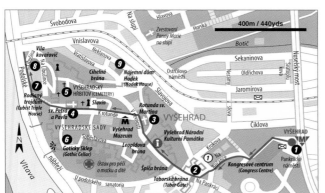

Above from left: the Cubist Triple House; autumn in Vinohrady.

Brick Gate
The other main entrance to the site apart from the Tábor Gate is the so-called 'Brick Gate' on Vratislavova. This is now an exhibition space where you can see the original Baroque statues from the Charles Bridge.

Below: Dvořak's gravestone in the Vyšehrad Cemetery.

VYŠEHRAD CEMETERY

Nearby lies the 1870 **Vyšehrad Cemetery** ❺ (Vyšehradský hřbitov; www. hrbitovy.cz), the resting place of national figures including the composers Smetana and Dvořák, the writers Jan Neruda and Karel Čapek, and the artist Alfons Mucha. A large monument, the **Slavín**, honours them all.

Legendary Statues

Pass through the stone gate opposite the cemetery and you will enter a wide lawn graced with four monumental statues by the sculptor Jan Myslbek. The statues depict characters from Czech legends including Libuše. Further along is the former summer palace of Emperor Charles IV. Also here is the **Gothic Cellar** ❻, home to a permanent exhibition on the history of the site.

There is wonderful view over the river and the city from the battlements. The remnants of buildings jutting out of the rock were once the outpost towers from which sentinels kept watch over the Vltava.

To descend to the embankment, return to the road in front of the cemetery and, near the medallion to the geologist Jan Krejčí, take the precipitous steps on the western side of the hill to the Vltava.

CUBIST HOUSES

As you descend you will pass above a splendid example of Cubist housing by the architect Josef Chochol (1880–1956). The **Cubist Triple House** ❼ (Rodinný trojdům) was built in 1913–14, soon after which Chochol abandoned the Cubist style he had adopted after studying with Otto Wagner in Vienna for Functionalist architecture.

At the bottom of the steps, on the corner of the Rašínovo nábřeží and Libušina, and nearby on Neklavova, are two more wonderful buildings by Chochol, the **Villa Kovařovič** ❽ (1912–13) and the **Hodek House** ❾ (Nájemní dům Hodek; 1913–14). Both fit graceful and well-proportioned façades into corner sites, the latter dramatically projecting from the hillside.

You can catch tram no. 17 back to the city centre from outside the villa.

VINOHRADY AND ŽIŽKOV

Cemeteries, science fiction and nationalist dreams all combine to give this journey through a couple of Prague's more run-down but fascinating areas a sense of discovery and adventure.

This route explores two of Prague's more interesting outer districts, the first the sometimes seedy district of run-down apartment blocks that is Žižkov (also known as Prague 3). Its working-class credentials are well established and it was at one time a hotbed of sedition. It is also famous for its huge number of basic local pubs (more than any other district of Prague), not all of which are welcoming or salubrious. The neighbouring district of Vinohrady gets its name from the vineyards that once thrived here. Today, in contrast to Žižkov it is rather bourgeois, pleasant, and lively, full of young, upwardly mobile Czechs, who live in the *fin-de-siècle* apartment blocks that make up much of the area.

ŽIŽKOV'S CEMETERIES

Begin the tour at the far-flung end of Žižkov by the **New Jewish Cemetery** ❶ (Židovské Hřbitovy; Mon–Thur and Sun, Oct–Mar 9am–4pm, Apr–Sept 9am–5pm, Fri 9am–1pm; male visitors must wear yarmulkes, skull-caps, which are available from the gatehouse; free). The cemetery is easily reached by metro, alighting at Želiv-

DISTANCE 5km (3 miles)
TIME A full day
START New Jewish Cemetery
END National Monument
POINTS TO NOTE
The first part of this tour is best taken by public transport – it would turn into quite a trek otherwise – and it is best to buy a 24-hour ticket that allows you to use the metro and trams for a whole day.

ského station, or you could take the tram (10, 11, 16, 19 and 26 all stop here). It is a serene and atmospheric spot with attractive, tree-lined avenues of graves overgrown with ivy. Looking at the headstones you realise just how wealthy and important the local Jewish community was before World War II. It included owners of industry to doctors and lawyers, and, ironically, many of them were German-speakers (most of the inscriptions are in either Hebrew or German).

Many people visit to see the grave of Franz Kafka, usually covered in flowers and notes (follow the signs leading you to block 21). However, the plain Cubist headstone is not the most

Above: Vinohrady's Husův Sbor Church; the New Jewish Cemetery is where the writer Franz Kafka is laid to rest.

Above from left:
Church of the Sacred Heart; New Jewish Cemetery; graffiti in Vinohrady; close-up of the 'babies' on the Television Tower.

impressive; look, for instance, for the striking Art Nouveau peacock on the headstone of painter Max Horb (in block 19).

Olšany Cemetery

Leave the New Jewish Cemetery and take either the metro to Flora station, or tram 10, 11 and 16 down to the stop of the same name. Here you will find the second of Žižkov's large cemeteries, **Olšany** ❷ (Hřbitov Olšany; www.hrbitovy.cz; Nov–Feb 8am–5pm, Mar–Apr and Oct 8am–6pm, May–Sept 8am–7pm; free). This huge necropolis has been the preferred burial spot of many famous Czechs (particularly if they have not managed to get a spot in Vyšehrad). Wonderfully Gothic in parts, it has higgledy piggledy graves, all slightly overgrown. Among the famous Czechs buried here are the painter Josef Mánes (1784–1843), the Art Nouveau Symbolist sculptor and architect František Bílek (1872–1941) and the painter and writer Josef Lada (1887–1957).

However, perhaps the most venerated grave is that of Jan Palach (1948–69), who committed suicide in political protest in 1969, and whose body was moved here in 1990. Palach is buried near the main entrance on Vinohradská. Also here is what must be one of the most overblown tombs, that of Rodina Hrdličkova: a sculptural group with a woman pleading with a man in uniform not to follow an angel up to heaven.

CHURCH OF THE SACRED HEART

Time to get back on public transport, this time to Jiřího z Poděbrad by metro or on the tram (again nos 10, 11 or 16). On the square of the same name as the metro station is the most unusual

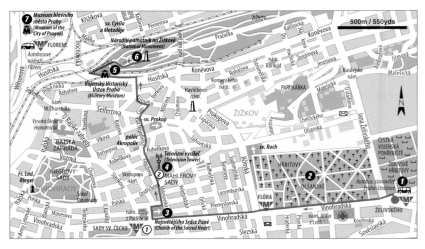

Modernist building in Prague, the **Church of the Sacred Heart ❸** (Nejsvětějšího Srdce Páně; open only for mass). Designed by the architect Josip Plečnik (who was responsible for the restoration of St Vitus; *see p.28*), it was built between 1928 and 1932, early considering its eclectic style that looks forward to the later developments of Postmodernism. The monolithic structure uses elements of Classical and Egyptian styles on what is a rather uncompromising exterior, and is impressive but not immediately appealing. However, it is enlivened by the huge glass clock on the narrow tower flanked by obelisks.

Church Interior

Unlike the forbidding façade, the interior is high and spacious with a coffered ceiling. The clock tower is climbed via a ramp that is double-sided so the light streams through from one side of the tower to the other; peering out through the glass faces gives a spectacular view over the city.

If you are hungry by now, take Nitranská leading south from the square to find a great little restaurant, **Mozaika**, see ⓘⓘ.

TELEVISION TOWER

Retrace your steps to the square and this time continue on foot, taking Milešovská at the northeast corner. This leads to Mahlerovy sady (Mahler Park) where, dominating the entire district and much of the city, is the **Prague Television Tower ❹** (Televizní vysílač Praha; tel: 242 418 778; www.tower.cz; daily 10am–11.30pm; charge). At 216m (708 ft) and with a boldly modern (almost science-fiction-inspired) design based on three interlocked towers, this is the most adventurous piece of architecture (by Václav Aulický and Jiří Kozák) of the

Local Pub
U vystřelenýho oka (U božich bojoníků 3; tel: 222 540 465; Mon–Sat 4.30pm–1am), the 'Shot-Out Eye', is one of the more welcoming pubs in Žižkov. Its name refers to the one-eyed Hussite hero Jan Žižkov, who gives his name to the district. The pub serves excellent beer in somewhat tatty surroundings, generally accompanied by loud music.

Food and Drink 🍴
ⓘ MOZAIKA
Nitranská 13; tel: 224 253 011; Mon–Fri 11.30am–midnight, Sat noon–midnight, Sun 4pm–midnight; €–€€
This friendly small restaurant has a clean, modern look and is worth a trip out even if you are not following the tour. The food is an eclectic mixture of Japanese, French and Italian dishes, steaks, salads and sushi. To sum it up, all tasty and at very reasonable prices.

Left: Prague Television Tower.

David Černý

Local artist David Černý has acquired a degree of notoriety with his often humorous and scatalogical works. For more examples of his past, and more recent, projects take a look at his amusing website (www.davidcerny.cz).

Communist era. Inspired by the similar tower on Alexanderplatz in Berlin, in an unpopular move it was built on the site of an old Jewish cemetery (used between 1786 and 1890).

Work began on construction in 1985, and the finishing touches were only made in 1991 after the fall of the Communist regime; before then it had allegedly been used for blocking foreign broadcasts from the West. Since then the tower has acquired a number of rather alien babies crawling up the steel tubes, courtesy of David Černý *(see margin left)*.

It is possible to take the lift up to the viewing platform at 93m (305ft), from where there is an awe-inspiring view over the entire city. The cube-like rooms suspended on the towers each have an annotated map pointing out what you can see, as well as an interesting series of photographs on the wall showing the construction of the tower. Below the viewing platform is a decent **restaurant**, see ⑪②, with the same astounding views.

Acropolis Palace

Easily visible from the tower (looking north) is a colourful apartment block on the nearby corner of Kubelíkova and Víta nejedléno. This is the **Acropolis Palace** (palác Akropolis; www.palacakropolis.cz), an arts centre set in the pre-war Akropolis theatre. The centre has a concert hall, cinema, theatre and exhibition space. Notable for putting on an eclectic selection of groups and acts, especially world music performers, this is one of Prague's more exciting music venues. You might also want to check out www.radio akropolis.cz for online streamed music.

ŽIŽKOV HILL

Make your way down the hill taking Víta nejedléno and Cimburkovo, turn left into Štítného and then go down Jeronýmova on to the main road of Husitská. Turn left, cross the road and just before the railway bridge take the cobbled road U památníku on the right.

Military Museum

On the way up the hill you will pass the **Military Museum** ❺ (Vojenský Historický Ústav Praha; tel: 973 204 913; www.vhu.cz; Tue–Sun 9.30am–6pm; free), which is rather more interesting than first impressions might suggest. The exhibits tell the story of the Czechoslovak Army from its inception in 1918 up to World War II and, apart from an impressive collection of headgear, there are good displays on World Wars I and II.

NATIONAL MONUMENT

Keep on climbing through the wooded park and you will come to a series of steps that lead up to a wide esplanade. Here you will find the **National Monument** ❻ (Národní památník), an immense granite-faced cube containing the Tomb of the Unknown Soldier (currently undergoing restoration and closed to the public).

Right in front of it stands one of the biggest equestrian statues in the world,

the monument to the Hussite leader Jan Žižka. The enormous equestrian statue (given greater height by being placed on a granite platform), by the Czech sculptor Bohumil Kafka (1878–1942), was commissioned after a competition in 1925 (one of a series that had created bad feeling and controversy about how to commemorate Žižka's victory). Only the Stalin monument, which had dominated Letná Hill until it was demolished in 1963, was bigger than that of Žižka.

The granite monolith of the National Monument itself was initially designed by Jan Zázvorka and built in 1929–30. However, after World War II the building was redesigned and used as both the Tomb of the Unknown Soldier and as a final resting place of worthies of the Communist Party, including Klement Gottwald, whose body was preserved in a similar way to that of Lenin in Red Square in Moscow. Gottwald is now in Olšany Cemetery *(see p.78)*. Although it is not possible to gain access at present, the legacy of the Communist redesign can be seen in the numerous reliefs and statues of heroic workers and revolutionary soldiers that adorn the bronze doors.

The complex now has a rather neglected air, and there are few other places in Prague where the ghost of the Communist years can be so easily felt. However, the walk up through the park is pleasant and the views from the top of the hill are wonderful.

To get back into town, retrace your steps down the hill and turn left into Husitská. At the first bus stop you come to (on U památníku), catch either no. 207 to Florenc, or 133 to Staroměstská.

CITY OF PRAGUE MUSEUM

Those who still have some energy left should alight at Florenc and make their way to Na Poříčí 51 and the **Museum of the City of Prague** ❼ (Muzeum hlavního músta Prahy; tel: 224 223 696; www.muzeumprahy.cz; Tue–Sun 9am–6pm; charge), a fascinating collection set in an imposing building. Much of the labelling is in Czech only, so ask to borrow the English booklet from the front desk.

The Collection

The galleries take you through the history of the city in great depth, from prehistory and the medieval period on the ground floor, to the Renaissance and Baroque upstairs. The museum's prize exhibit is undoubtably Antonín Langweil's enormous paper model of the city made between 1826 and 1837. Also here is the architect Josef Mánes's original design for the astrological face of the Old Town Hall.

Above from far left: Acropolis Palace; the revolutionary bronze doors of the National Monument; the immense statue of Jan Žižkov at the National Monument.

Food and Drink 🍴

② **RESTAURACE A SALÓNEK**
Mahlerovy sady 1; tel: 267 005 778; daily 11am–11pm; €€
This restaurant is 66m (216ft) up the Žižkov Television Tower. The food is reasonable – a selection of international dishes – and the draught beer is remarkably cheap, but what really sells it is the extraordinary view you get over the city.

MUSEUM OF MODERN ART

The district of Holešovice started as a farming hamlet, then later, in 1884, was incorporated into Prague as an industrial suburb. Today, however, it is a fixture on the tourist map by virtue of its art museum.

Church of St Antony

Built in 1908–14, the towers of this substantial church (Mon–Fri noon–7pm, Sat 7am–noon, Sun 7am–noon and 5–7pm; free) are derived from those on the Týn Church in Staré Město. Inside, there is an imposing altar surrounded by a frieze, and elegant plain columns along the nave that sprout into neo-Gothic vaulting. As well as some good *fin-de-siècle* stained glass, there is also an interesting fake grotto, dripping with stalactites.

DISTANCE 0.8km (½ mile) not including distance at the museum
TIME 2–3 hours
START Church of St Antony
END Veletržní Palace
POINTS TO NOTE
The museum is closed on Mon. Holešovice is served by trams 5, 12, 14 and 17 and by metro.

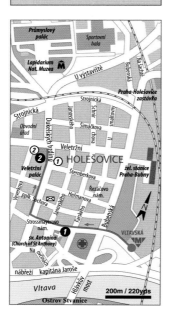

Emerging from the main exit of the shabby metro station of Vltavská, turn right (west) and walk up Antonínská (crossing over Bubenská) to Holešovice district's main square, Strossmayerovo náměstí. On your left is the large **Church of St Antony ❶** (Sv. Antonína; *see margin, left*), while the cobbled square in front forms the meeting point for several major tram lines. From the end of the square, turn right onto Dukelských hrdinů and walk down the hill, perhaps stopping for a cream cake at the delicatessen on the way, see Ⓨ①. After a few minutes you come to the art museum on your left at no. 47. Just before you go in, look further down the hill and you can see in the distance the Průmyslový Palace *(see opposite)*.

ART MUSEUM

The **Veletržní Palace ❷** (Veletržní palác; tel: 224 301 024; Tue–Sun 10am–6pm; www.ngprague.cz; charge), or Trade Fair Palace, is one of the earliest large-scale Functionalist buildings in Europe. It was designed by Oldřich Tyl and Josef Fuchs to house exhibitions to show off Czech industrial expertise and built between 1925 and 1929. It was

used for industrial exhibitions until 1951, then as the offices for foreign trade companies until 1974, when it was badly damaged in a fire. It was rebuilt in 1995 and ever since has housed the National Gallery's collections of 19th-, 20th- and 21st-century art.

Practicalities

At the time of writing, however, the permanent exhibition was undergoing reorganisation, with the 19th-century Czech collection now transferred from the fourth floor here to St George's Basilica in Hradčany *(see p.28)*. The route around the museum described below should, even so, still be valid.

As you enter, on the left is an excellent art bookshop. Just beyond the ticket desks are lockers for stowing your coats and bags, and at the far end of the ground floor, near the stairs and lifts, is a café, see ①②. Begin the tour by taking the lift to the third floor.

Czech Art 1900–30

The first space in the galleries on the third floor is given over to the works of František Kupka (1871–1957). They span from his early Symbolist paintings such as *The Path of Silence I* (1903), to those in the Fauvist style, such as *Family Portrait* (1910), via the transitional *Two-Colour Fugue – Amorpha* (1912), to his later outright abstraction, as in *Vertical Planes III* (1912–13) and the De Stijl-like *Series CVI* (1935–6).

Next are the experimental photographic works of František Drtikol (1883–1961), with their Art Deco feel. Then there is the Cubism at which

Czech artists so excelled. Look out for Emil Filla's *Salome* (1911–12) and the unsurpassed Cubist furniture and ceramics of Josef Gočár (1880–1945) and Pavel Janák (1882–1956). Another luminary of the Czech avant-garde, Bohumil Kubišta, seems – strangely given his name – more Futurist than Cubist (see *Meditation*, 1915). In contrast, the works of Gutfreund, Čapek and Špála seem less convincing and were already dated by the time they were produced.

Things tend to degenerate from here on, but the sculptures of Karel Dvořák (1893–1950) are interesting in their sense of social purpose. See especially the engaging *To America* (1925), depicting an emigrating couple asleep on a bench.

Other exhibits of particular interest in this section of the museum are those related more to design than high art. There are many fascinating works in the genres of book illustration, stage design, fashion, architecture, aircraft design and furniture. Look out in particular for the models, drawings and

Průmyslový Palác
The Výstaviště exhibition ground includes the huge Průmyslový palác, which was built for the Exhibition of 1891. The palace is covered in tour 13 *(see p.86)*. Designed by František Prášil and Bedřich Münzberger, it was one of the first Art Nouveau buildings in Prague, and is still used for trade fairs and exhibitions. Also in the grounds of the Výstaviště, behind the main exhibition hall, is the recently restored Panorama (daily 10am–5pm; charge) which houses a huge 19th-century painting, *The Battle of Lipany*, 1434 by Luděk Marold (1865–98).

Food and Drink

① LIBEŘSKÉ LAHŮDKY
Dukelských hrdinů 33; tel: 233 374 995; Mon–Sat 9am–7pm; €
Delicatessen serving open sandwiches, filled rolls, cooked meats, schnitzels, salads and excellent cakes and pastries. Very inexpensive.

② MUSEUM RESTAURANT
Ground floor, Veletržní palác; opening times as for museum; €
This restaurant is dirt-cheap, egalitarian and, most of all, basic. It serves open sandwiches, soups and other unreconstructed Communist rations. The daily hot dish is sustaining, even if redolent of school dinners.

Backhanded Compliment
The Trade Fair Palace housing the Museum of Modern Art was admired by Le Corbusier, who saw in it how his own large-scale projects might be realised. However, he qualified his enthusiasm by saying, 'It's an interesting building but it's not yet architecture.'

photographs of the architects Aldolf Loos and Ludvík Kysela, whose fully realised works you can see on other tours in this book (see tour 15 for the Müller Villa, for example, or walk 8 for the architecture of Wenceslas Square).

French Art

The highlight of the museum for many people will be the galleries of French art, which are also on the third floor. Thanks to state acquisitions of major collections in 1923 and 1960, and numerous individual acquisitions in between, hardly any major French painter from the mid-19th to early 20th century is not represented here.

The displays begin with busts by Rodin, three small pictures by Delacroix and a couple of paintings by Corot – *Young Shepherds among the Rocks* (1842) and *Farm Dwelling in the Woods* (1873). The gallery also contains fine examples of the work of Courbet, notably *Woman in a Straw Hat with Flowers* (1857) and *Forest Grotto* (c.1865).

The Impressionists are particularly well represented, especially by Pissarro (*In the Kitchen Garden*, 1881), and *Garden at Val Hermeil*, 1880) and Sisley (*The Bridge at Sèvres*, 1877, and *Bourgogne Lock at Moret*, 1882). There are also a couple of early works by Monet: *Orchard Trees in Blossom* (1879) and *Women among Flowers* (1875). The academic side of Degas can be seen in his *Portrait of Lorenzo Pagans* (1882), and there is a slightly sentimental picture by Renoir, *The Lovers* (1875).

Toulouse-Lautrec's picture of two women dancing together, *At the Moulin Rouge* (1892), is a fine example of the artist's output. There is also a strong showing of Gauguin's work – look out in particular for *Flight* (1902). Van Gogh is represented by the vibrant canvas *Green Wheat* (1889). Perhaps most impressive all, though, is the group of 19 works by Picasso, from the early *Seated Female Nude* (1906) to a wide range of his Cubist paintings.

The gallery has three outstanding works by Cézanne: *Portrait of Joachim Gasquet* (1896–7), *House in Aix-en-Provence* (1885–7) and *Fruits* (1879–82). There are also pictures by Rousseau and Seurat (note his *Port of Honfleur*, 1881) and Braque and Derain, including the wonderful *Cadaquès* (1910) and *Montreuil-sur-Mer* (also 1910).

Also present are works by Despiau, Dufy, Chagall and Bourdelle. Matisse is represented by a series of his lithographs as well as by the intriguing *Joaquine* (1910). At the end of the collection, be sure to look out for Maillol's beautiful chalk drawing, *Female Nude* (1902).

Art from 1930 to the Present Day

The collections on the second floor begin with a welcome invitation to sit down in a little cinema in a side room. Here, there is a display celebrating the work of the master puppeteer and animator Jiří Trnka (1912–69), sometimes described as the 'Disney of the East'. There are also screenings of extracts from classic Czech films.

Czech artists made a distinctive contribution to Surrealism, and are represented in the succeeding galleries by Jindřich Štyrský (1899–1942), by

the female artist who went under the name of Toyen (1902–80), and by the bizarre illuminated sculptures of Zdeněk Pešánek (1896–1965).

The grimness of the wartime Occupation is expressed in works by the artists of Group 42. Works such as *Railroad Station with a Windmill* by František Hudeček (b.1909) combine the artistic innovations of the previous decades with a fascination with industry and technology.

The post-war landscape looked hardly less optimistic. After 1948, Socialist Realism was the only recognised artistic creed. Art became divided into the official and unofficial, and any artists deemed to be either 'individualists' or 'formalists' were driven underground. The situation is well illustrated in the next few sections of the gallery. There is a small display of Socialist-Realist paintings (most of the gallery's holdings of art of this type languish in disgrace in store). Then there are much larger spaces devoted to artists who worked outside the official ideology. One area where, exceptionally, the official channels for creativity did engender some inspiration was that of industrial and domestic design: a display of items sent to the Brussels Expo of 1958 – in cluding glass, ceramics and furniture – shows work at the forefront of its field.

20th-Century Foreign Art

On the first floor is the collection of Foreign Art, which has particular strength and depth in Austrian and German Expressionist art. Among the finest examples from this movement

are *Operation* (1912) by Max Oppenheimer, *Pregnant Woman and Death* (1911) by Egon Schiele, and *Portrait of the Poet Albert Ehrenstein* (1913–14) by Oskar Kokoschka. Kokoschka's townscapes of Prague painted in 1934–5 are also displayed nearby. In this context, look out too for the earlier, proto-Expressionist works by Edvard Munch: *Dancing on a Shore* (1900) and *Seashore Landscape near Lübeck* (1907).

Moving on, there are two fine Secessionist works by Gustav Klimt – *Virgin* (1913) and *Castle with Moat* (1908–9) – and two large Cubist-inspired paintings by Aristarkh Lentulov: *A Ballet Theme* (1912) and *Landscape near Kislovodsk* (1913). Meanwhile, Paul Klee's mesmerising *Tropical Forest* (1915) is difficult to fit into any established art-historical category.

Thereafter, the collection is patchy in its continuation of the story of 20th-century art, although there are pieces by Miró and Picasso, Henry Moore, Joseph Beuys and Antoni Tàpies. And even if the quality of the collection is uneven, it sharpens the impression the few masterpieces make to have them displayed next to less-inspired works.

When you have finished, repair to the pub across the road from the museum for refreshments, see .

Above: one of the gallery's upper floors.

Temporary Exhibitions

If you have time to spare, visit one of the temporary exhibitions elsewhere in the museum. Recent offerings have included the triennial show of contemporary art and a selection of Modigliani's finest works.

Food and Drink

③ **RESTAURACE U HOUBAŘE**
Dukelských hrdinů 30; tel: 222 982 430; Mon–Sun 11am–midnight; €
Straightforward pub, serving simple Czech food – fried cheese, pork steaks, dumplings – and Pilsner Urquellto to a regular crowd. The walls are adorned with basic-looking rustic implements.

VÝSTAVIŠTĚ TO TROJA

This full-day tour contains quite a bit of walking, much of it through parkland, and it takes you from a huge Art Nouveau exhibition hall to a Baroque château and a modern greenhouse.

Above from far left: exterior, frieze and bust at the Průmyslový Palace, Výstaviště's main exhibition hall; waterlilies, Stromovka.

Holešovice
The district of Holešovice, to the east of Výstaviště, was incorporated into the city in 1884. It is now a little run-down, but it does have quite a number of elegant, intricately decorated late 19th-century apartment buildings.

> **DISTANCE** 4km (2½ miles)
> **TIME** A full day
> **START** Průmyslový Palace
> **END** Prague Botanical Garden
> **POINTS TO NOTE**
> Note that this tour visits the area just to the north of the one covered in tour 12, so an option might be to combine the two, albeit by flitting past some sights to fit everything in. There are very few decent places in which to eat and drink on the way to Troja; in summer there is a café in the palace grounds, a stall outside the zoo and another stall in the botanical garden, but that is all. A better option is to take food and drink with you, as the Stromovka park is a great place for a picnic. It's also a lovely place for children to run around, which, coupled with a trip to the zoo, makes this a good tour to do with kids.

The northern reaches of the city are often ignored by tourists, but contain important sights such as one of Prague's first Art Nouveau buildings, a fine Baroque palace and the city's Botanical Garden.

VÝSTAVIŠTĚ EXHIBITION GROUND

Dominating the view down the long street of Dukelských hrdinů *(see p.82)* is the huge and ornate **Průmyslový Palace ❶** (Průmyslový palác), part of the Výstaviště Exhibition Ground. Designed by František Prášil and Bedřich Münzberger, it was constructed for the Exhibition of 1891. One of the very first Art Nouveau buildings in Prague, it is still used for trade fairs and exhibitions – which vary hugely, from the mundane to the erotic – but when there is no show on it can appear a little strange and bleak.

To the rear of the main exhibition hall is the Křižík Fountain, designed by the electrical pioneer František Křižík. A masterpiece of kitsch, the fountain comprises hundreds of individually controlled jets and lights, all set to music.

The Lapidarium

To the right of the Průmyslový Palace, in one of the side pavilions, is the National Museum's **Lapidarium ❷** (tel: 233 375 636; www.nm.cz; Tue–Fri noon–6pm, Sat–Sun 10am–6pm; charge). This, a Bohemian stone-sculpture collection of the 11th to 19th

centuries, contains some of the most important statues that at one time decorated the city. The Lapidarium is currently closed for – in that common Czech term – 'technical reasons', and there are no hints as to when it will reopen; keep your eye on the website for further information.

However, the items the museum holds are well worth a look when it does reopen. Among the Romanesque and Gothic exhibits one of the finest is the original of the bronze equestrian statue of St George, which originally stood outside St Vitus (now replaced by a copy; *see p.28*). Also here is the original tympanum from the Týn Church (1380–90), Petr Parléř's exceptional figures from the Old Town Bridge Tower, as well as the original pillar and statue of the Bruncvík.

The Renaissance exhibits are dominated by the Krocín fountain that used to stand in Staroměstské náměstí. And the Baroque pieces include the original (earlier) equestrian statue of St Wenceslas from Wenceslas Square as well as a series of interesting gilded and brightly painted statues.

The remainder of the collection is given over to works from the 19th century. Notable among these are the two tombs made by Václav Prachner and the four allegorical groups designed for the cupola of the National Museum by Bohuslav Schnirch.

The Panorama

Also in the grounds of Výstaviště, behind the main exhibition hall, is the newly restored **Panorama ❸** (Apr–

Oct Tue–Fri 2–5pm, Sat–Sun 10am–5pm; charge). Panoramas were very popular during the 19th century – especially of subjects that portrayed patriotic themes – and this huge circular painting by Luděk Marold (1865–98) depicts *The Battle of Lipany, 1434.*

Below: the Lapidarium showcases Bohemian stone sculpture dating from the 11th to 19th centuries.

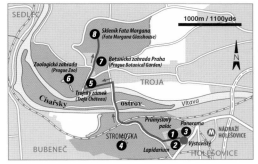

STROMOVKA PARK

To the left of the main entrance to Výstaviště is the way into **Stromovka** ❹. Previously a royal hunting ground, this wooded park became a public space at the beginning of the 19th century and is one of the most extensive open spaces in the city. A signposted foot- and cycle-path leads through the park towards the Troja château. A turn-off to the right takes you under the railway line and over a footbridge to Císařský ostrov (Emperor's Island). The path continues straight across the island, to the left of the Czech Equestrian Federation, to an elegant modern footbridge. On the other side turn left along the river and then right onto on U trojského zámku.

TROJA CHÂTEAU

Here is the entrance to the **Troja Château** ❺ (Trojský zámek; tel: 283 851 614; www.ghmp.cz; Tue–Thur, Sun 10am–6pm, Fri 1–7pm, Sat 10am–7pm; charge; the Trojská karta, www.trojskakarta.cz, gives you access to the château, zoo and botanical garden, *see opposite*). The building is set in large formal gardens, one of the main attractions of the site, part of which is a large apple orchard.

Built between 1679 and 1685 by Jean-Baptiste Mathey for Václav Vojtěch of Sternberg, this large Baroque mansion has an ornate interior covered in frescoes on Classical themes (not greatly enhanced by a bodged restoration). The château and gardens suffered greatly in the 2002 floods, but much of the damage has now been repaired. Approaching through the gardens does give you a view of the southern façade, with its staircase decorated by monumental sculpture representing the battle between the gods and Titans.

The Interior
When you enter the building, you will be given a pair of overshoes, designed to protect the floors. The château is home to a collection of 19th-century Czech painting, the highlights of which are probably the landscapes on display in the first few rooms. Many of the same artists are represented as in the National Gallery's collection of 19th-century art *(see p.28)*; of particular interest are Ludvík Kohl's highly Romantic *Gothic Hall with a Meeting of a Secret Brotherhood* (1812); two lovely landscapes of mountain waterfalls by Charlotta Peipenhagenová (1880s); a *Forest Scene* (1853) by Josef Mánes; and the virtuoso *Path in a Deciduous Forest* by Bedřich Havránek (1878).

The rooms upstairs are particularly wonderfully decorated, especially the Grand Hall, which is covered in frescoes by Abraham Godyn (1663–1724).

PRAGUE ZOO

Just outside the Troja Château is the stop for the no. 112 bus, behind which is the entrance to **Prague Zoo** ❻ (Zoologická zahrada; U Trojského zámku 3; tel: 296 112 111; www.zoopraha.cz; Mar 9am–5pm, Apr,

Classical Concerts
Music concerts are occasionally held at the Grand Hall in the Troja Château. Check its website for details.

May, Sept, Oct 9am–6pm, Jun, Jul, Aug 9am–7pm, Nov, Dec, Jan ,Feb 9am–4pm). The zoo was particularly badly affected by the 2002 flood, when there were tragic scenes of the animals trying to cope with the rising waters.

PRAGUE BOTANICAL GARDEN

From the zoo, head further uphill, taking the footpath that leads off right from the road that climbs the hill above the château. A sign points you towards the Botanická zahrada Praha. At the top turn left to find the main entrance to **Prague Botanical Garden ❼** (Botanická zahrada Praha; tel: 603 582 191; www.botanicka.cz; daily: Apr 9am–6pm, May–Sept 9am–7pm, Oct 9am–5pm, Nov–Mar 9am–4pm; charge).

The gardens are very extensive and include, among other things, a Mediterranean and Japanese garden, medicinal and poisonous plants, as well as a perennial flower bed. Also attached to the garden, cascading down the hill towards the château, is the St Clara vineyard. The view from the top of the hill by the St Clara chapel is lovely.

Fata Morgana
Following the road up to the right of the main entrance brings you to the curving **Fata Morgana Glasshouse ❽** (Skleník Fata Morgana; Tue–Sun, same times as the gardens). Divided into three main sections – semi-desert, tropical rainforest and cloud forest – it is now well established and the plants are flourishing. From the dry zone a sub-terranean passage leads through a divided pool, one side for the Americas, the other for Africa and Asia, before emerging into the hot and steamy tropics – very green, with huge tropical butterflies flitting amongst the plants. However, perhaps even more interesting is the cooler cloud-forest room, where jets provide a constant mist of water. Above, the glasshouse footpaths lead through an attractive woodland with picnic and play areas.

To get back into town, return to the bus stop outside the zoo entrance and take the no. 112 to Nádraží Holešovice metro station.

Above from far left: Troja Château; the Fata Morgana Glasshouse at the Botanical Garden.

Below: leafy Stromovka is popular with cyclists.

SMÍCHOV

Visit Smíchov for the Mozart Museum – representing the district's 18th-century heritage of aristocratic summer retreats – and then for the Staropramen Brewery – recalling its 19th-century history as an industrial working-class enclave.

DISTANCE 2km (1¼ miles)
TIME A half-day
START Andel metro station
END Staropramen Brewery
POINTS TO NOTE
For guided tours of the Staropramen Brewery, telephone ahead or book via the website *(see p.92)*.

The route begins on your arrival at **Anděl metro station ❶**. This station was built as a Communist showpiece and used to be known as Moskevská (Moscow) – a gesture of friendship towards the Soviet Union, and a point hammered home with a number of large murals showing triumphant workers striding into the future. Opposite the platforms, you can still see today eight bronze reliefs, one showing two cosmonauts, another with a young girl waving flags marked 'Moskva' and 'Praha'.

Ascending the escalators, you emerge, ironically, into the Nový Smíchov Shopping Centre, a showpiece of the new capitalist Prague and the city's largest, flashiest mall. The name 'Anděl' means 'angel', and so the centre's architect, Jean Nouvel, has had a 21st-century angel depicted on the glass façade, along with quotations (in red writing) from Czech literature, including from the works of Franz Kafka.

BERTRAMKA VILLA

The Approach

As you exit the building, make your way west up Plzeňská, along the side of the shopping centre. Just behind it, on the corner of Stroupežnického, is an interesting synagogue, the Smíchovská Synagoga. Founded in 1863, it was given a Modernist makeover in 1931 by Leopolda Ehrmanna and then completely renovated and reopened in 2004 (with an excellent second-hand bookshop attached). Continuing up the road, you pass under a flyover and then bear left off Plzeňská onto Kartouzská, which shortly, near the corporate-

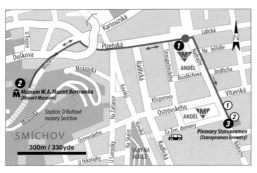

looking Mövenpick Hotel, transforms into Mozartova. Follow this leafy lane uphill and on your right is the gateway to the **Mozart Museum** ❷ (Muzeum W.A. Mozarta Bertramka; tel: 257 318 461; www.bertramka.com; daily Apr–Oct 9am–6pm, Nov–Mar 9.30am–4pm; charge).

The Villa

Once a vineyard manor house, the property later became the country villa of František Dušek and his young wife (he was old enough to be her father), the singer Josefina Dušková. It was here that Mozart stayed on his visits to Prague in 1787 and 1791, and here that he composed the aria 'Bella mia fiamma, addio' from *Don Giovanni* for Josefina. He also, allegedly, scrawled out the overture to the opera the night before its première at the Estates Theatre *(see p.122)* in the city centre. Sadly, the original villa was largely destroyed by fire on New Year's Eve 1872–3. It was finally reconstructed in 1941.

The villa regularly holds concerts of Mozart's music (see the website for details), at which times the museum café opens late especially.

The Museum

The building itself now functions as a museum. The first room has a cabinet of instruments, including an early clarinet and a basset horn – which Mozart

Above from far left: Bertramka Villa; sign on the side of the Staropramen Brewery; bright Smíchov flowers.

Church Square
The barn-like Church of St Václav, on Štefánikova, was built between 1881 and 1885 to designs by Antonín Barvitius. Behind it is the small park of náměstí 14 října. On the northern side of the square, beside the church, is the Portheimka, a small 18th-century mansion built by Kilián Ignáz Dientzenhofer (one of the architects of St Nicholas's Church in nearby Malá Strana) as his town residence.

Left: Mozart stamps at the Bertramka Villa.

Above from left:
the Staropramen
Brewery; watering the
grass at the Bertramka
Villa; tram lines at the
Transport Museum;
trams as they used
to make them.

Above: Mozart's
piano at the
Bertramka Villa;
Mozart bust.

Industrial Heyday

Smíchov was
incorporated into the
city of Prague in 1838
and soon afterwards
became a focal
point of Czech
industrialisation.
Associated with this
economic growth was
the building of a new
railway station, the
Smíchovské nádraží
in the south of the
district. Built in 1854,
it was revamped in
1947 to designs by
Jan Zázvorka and
Jan Žák with an
imposing Socialist-
Realist façade.

was chiefly responsible for introducing to the orchestra.

In the next room is a real piece of Mozartiana, an elegant fortepiano by Ignatz Kober (Vienna, 1785–6), one of only three such instruments to survive. Legend has it that Mozart played on this instrument in Prague in January 1787. Close by is a hammer piano (1807–10) used in the filming of *Amadeus*. To complete the trio of keyboard instruments, towards the end of the exhibition is a large harpsichord, made in 1722, and the only surviving example by Johann Heinrich Gräbner of Dresden.

The museum's walls are lined with illustrations and documents, which build up an interesting picture of Prague during Mozart's time. On the more kitsch side is a small glass tablet encasing a lock of Mozart's hair. You can also see photographs of the numerous famous musical visitors, such as Tchaikovsky, Vincent d'Indy and Leoš Janáček, who later came to pay homage at this Mozart shrine on their visits to Prague.

THE BREWERY

Returning to Anděl metro station again, now make your way south, down Nádražní to the enormous **Staropramen Brewery** ❸ (Pivovary Staropramen; tel: 257 191 402; www.pivovary-staropramen.cz) at no. 84. Attached to the brewery is a pub and restaurant serving, of course, extremely good beer, see ⑪①. It is also possible to see the inside of the brewery, with guided tours daily (one or two in English each day), usually around lunchtime or early afternoon. Entrance is via the doorway on Pivovarská on the east side.

The Tour

The hour-long tours begin with a short film outlining Staropramen's history from its construction in 1869 to its takeover by the Belgian group Interbrew in 2000. Visitors then proceed to Brewhouse no. 1, where the first stages in beer production are demonstrated, followed by Brewhouse no. 5, which exhibits the fermentation and ageing processes, filtration, bottling and quality control, and finally a visit to the New Brewhouse. The tour ends with a beer-tasting session. If after that, however, you are still thirsty (or perhaps hungry), then repair to an old-fashioned Smíchov pub nearby, see ⑪②.

Food and Drink 🍴

① POTREFENÁ HUSA NA VERANDÁCH
Nádražní 84; tel: 257 191 200;
Mon–Sat 11am–midnight; €
Smart, modern bar-restaurant offering 10 varieties of beer alongside traditional high-carb Czech food to soak up the alcohol. Good value.

② HOSTINEC U VÁHY
Nádražní 88; tel: 257 326 539;
Mon–Fri 10am–11pm, Sat–Sun noon–10pm; €
This unaffected working-man's pub serves Gambrinus beer so you can perform a 'compare and contrast' with Staropramen's product next door. Serves good honest grub as well.

TRANSPORT MUSEUM AND MÜLLER VILLA

Although this tour has to be planned in advance, it is well worth thinking ahead, as the Müller Villa is one of the least-known and most rewarding sights in all of Prague.

This tour is short, but includes one of the city's most worthwhile sights for anyone interested in the history of art and design. First a transport museum gives an overview of how the city's exemplary public transport developed over the past 100 years or more, while the latter half of the tour takes you around a gem of Modernist design.

TRANSPORT MUSEUM

Begin at the Vozovna Střešovice tram stop (trams nos 1, 2, 18 and 22 will bring you here). This is just outside the **Public Transport Museum** ❶ (Muzeum městské hromadné dopravy; tel: 296 124 900; www.dpp.cz; mid-Mar–mid-Nov Sat–Sun 9am–5pm; charge). Set in an old tram shed, this is also where the 'nostalgic' tram no. 91 begins and ends its journey *(see margin right and www. dpp.cz for details)*.

The Collection

The museum's collection of trams and trolleybuses outlines the history of public transport in the city, from a horse-drawn tram car dating from 1886 to a bus dating from 1985. Some of the early trams are beautifully made and decorated in Art Nouveau style, and

DISTANCE 1km (⅔ mile)
TIME A half-day
START Public Transport Museum
END Müller Villa
POINTS TO NOTE

There is nowhere to eat en route, but this tour is relatively short and the tram service quick and frequent, so it is best to eat in town before you set off or after the tour has finished. Note that the transport museum is only open at weekends, while the Müller Villa is also open on Tue and Thur but must be booked in advance *(see p.94 for further details and contact numbers)*.

'Nostalgic' Tram 91
Every year the Transport Museum runs one of its old trams along a city-centre route, taking in a number of main sights. The route varies each year but generally it runs from the museum in Střešovice to the Výstaviště exhibition ground via Malá Strana, the National Theatre, Wenceslas Square and Náměstí republicky. The trip takes about 40 mins, leaving on the hour from midday; there is a 20-min wait, then the tram makes its way back to the museum.

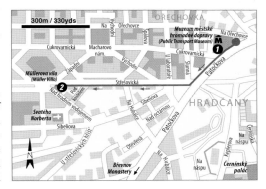

Above: the Müller Villa; Karlštejn Castle.

there is a good exhibition showing the building of the city's metro system.

MÜLLER VILLA

Just around the corner, at Nad hradním vodojemem 14, is the **Müller Villa** ❷ (Müllerova vila; tel: 224 312 012; www.mullerovavila.cz; admission only on guided tours that must be booked in advance, Tue, Thur, Sat–Sun: Apr–Oct 9am, 11am, 1pm, 3pm and 5pm, Nov–Mar 10am, noon, 2pm and 4pm; charge), the only example of the work of architect Adolf Loos *(see box below)* in Prague. The villa was designed and built between 1928 and 1930 for the wealthy couple František and Milada Müller. As befits an iconic Modernist building, the exterior is plain and severe, but the beautifully designed interiors are luxurious.

The tour, limited to around seven people at a time, is very informative and lasts around one hour. It takes you around all the public and private areas of the villa. Even the heating system and utility rooms show just how well-integrated Loos' design was: next door to the boiler room is the laundry, with long racks that pull out to dry the clothes using the heat from the boiler for both the hot water and drying.

Now the villa has been restored to its former glory it is possible to see just how well laid-out the building is and how colour is used as an element in the organisation of the overall design. Particularly appealing elements are the open-plan living room with its large windows and a dining space above, the 'boudoir', a cosy space that acted as a private retreat, and the elegant lady's dressing room.

Adolf Loos

One of the most important architects of early Modernism, Adolf Loos was born in Brno in 1870, then part of the Austro-Hungarian empire. He trained in Vienna and, after a short period in North America, soon established a reputation as an iconoclast, particularly following the publication of his most influential work, *Ornament and Crime,* in 1908. This outlined his ideas on decoration (he repudiated it), and these were put into effect in one of his most important buildings, the Michaeler House (1909–11) in Vienna. The blank, featureless façade was revolutionary and even raised the ire of the emperor, who had to look out on it from the Hofburg. He carried these ideas over into the construction of domestic architecture, notably in the Steiner House (Vienna, 1910) and the Müller Villa in Prague. He died near Vienna in 1933.

KARLŠTEJN

If you're feeling a little claustrophic in Prague, make an excursion, by train or car, to Karlštejn Castle. Traipse round the castle, picnic by the river, drink a beer in a pub, and then have a snooze on the journey home.

Some 30km (19 miles) southwest of Prague, in a romantic forested setting, is Karlštejn Castle (tel: 311 681 617; www.hradkarlstejn.cz; Tue–Sun: Mar 9am–noon, 1–3pm, Apr and Oct 9am–noon, 1–4pm, May–June and Sept 9am–noon, 12.30–5pm, July–Aug 9am–noon, 12.30–6pm; charge).

History

The castle was built between 1348 and 1365, possibly under the direction of Matthew of Arras, first architect of St Vitus's Cathedral in Prague; it was modified during Renaissance times and then fell into near decay. Magnificent as it is, much of what we see today is a zealous late-19th-century reconstruction by the conservation architect Josef Mocker, who attempted to return the castle to its original Gothic appearance.

REACHING THE CASTLE

If you arrive by train, it is an easy 10-minute walk from **Karlštejn station** across the bridge to the village. From there, continue along the main street to make the steep ascent to the castle (a further 15-minute walk).

Lunch Options

For those arriving in Karlštejn at midday, you may wish to take lunch

> **DISTANCE** 60km (38 miles) rtn
> **TIME** A half-day
> **START** Prague
> **END** Karlštejn Castle
> **POINTS TO NOTE**
>
> Trains from Prague leave the main railway station (Hlavní nádraží) approximately every hour from about 8am (journey time approx. 45 mins). Alternatively, take metro line B to Smíchovské nádraží, and catch a train there. If travelling by car, take the E50–D5 (Route 5) towards Plzeň, leave the motorway at exit 10 (at Loděnice) and follow the signs to Karlštejn. Note that Karlštejn Castle's Tour 2 *(see p.97)* needs to be booked in advance.

Rich Surroundings
The limestone (karst) landscape in which Karlštejn is set is characterised by forests rich in wildlife, numerous lakes, and fissures and caverns. Some 12km (7 miles) to the west, the caves at Koněprusy were employed as work-shops by medieval counterfeiters.

at one of the village's restaurants, see ⑪①. Alternatively, bring a picnic to eat on the banks of the Berounka River, or buy some comestibles at the grocery store, **Potraviny** (Mon–Sat

Food and Drink
① U JANŮ
Main Street, Karlštejn 90; tel: 311 681 210; daily 9.30am–10pm; €€
Standard Czech fare of acceptable quality at acceptable prices. Terrace in the shade of the trees for dining outside. Be aware that there is live music at weekends.

A trip to Karlštejn can easily be combined with a visit to the castle at Křivoklát (tel: 313 558 120; www.krivoklat.cz), about 40 minutes further along the same railway line beyond Beroun. The castle, founded in 1109, has everything a medieval fortress should have: towers and spires, Gothic interiors, hunting trophies, an ancient library (52,000 volumes), a working smithy, dungeons and a torture chamber (with iron maiden). Křivoklát is also usually much less crowded than Karlštejn.

8am–5pm), on your right as you walk up the main street towards the castle. In peak season it may be preferable, though, to time your visit so as to arrive earlier in the morning, before the coach parties arrive.

Castle Walls

As you approach **Karlštejn Castle** ❶ (Hrad Karlštejn) itself, you can appreciate the massive walls and protruding cliffs that made it impregnable to attack throughout its history. However, Emperor Charles IV, for whom Karlštejn was built, did not intend the castle to be a military stronghold; strategically speaking it would have served no useful purpose. Instead, he had it built solely to safeguard the holy relics and coronation insignia of the kingdom.

Holy Relics

During medieval times the holy relics housed within the castle were of huge significance: they included what are said to be two thorns from Jesus's crown, a fragment of the sponge soaked in vinegar and offered to him on the cross, one of St John the Baptist's teeth and the arm of St Anne. To possess such treasures was seen as a sign of God's favour, a blessing for the emperor and his subjects. The collection of relics was presented twice a year for public worship: on the Friday after Easter, the Day of the Holy Relics, and on 29 November, the anniversary of Charles IV's death. Mass is still celebrated in the Chapel of the Cross, where the precious items are conserved.

CASTLE INTERIOR

To see inside the castle, visitors must join one of the two guided tours (both available in a number of languages). Tour 1 concentrates on the Imperial Palace, Tour 2 on the library and

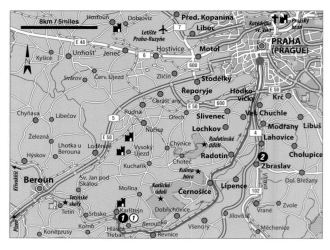

chapels, including the Chapel of the Holy Cross.

Tour 1

This tour explores the interiors of the Imperial Palace and the lower floors of the Marian Tower. These include the Great Hall, the Audience Chamber and the private apartments of the emperor and his wife, which are decorated with furnishings from the 14th to the 19th century. Then there is the Treasury and Jewel Hall, where you can see treasures from the Chapel of the Holy Cross, as well as a replica of the St Wenceslas Crown. You will also be taken to view the former castle prison. The tour lasts about an hour.

Tour 2

This second option lasts about 100 minutes and is only available from June to October. Crucially, it also needs to be booked in advance (tel: 274 008 154/5/6) – an effort that is well worth making, since it will allow you access to one of the most illustrious medieval sanctuaries on the continent, the Chapel of the Holy Cross.

The tour also takes in the Marian and Great towers before proceeding to the library, with its heavily ornamented interior and exhibition on Karlštejn's reconstruction. It also visits the Church of Our Lady, in which Charles's court painter, Nikolaus Wurmser, portrayed the emperor with the relics of the Passion beneath a heaven filled with the angelic host. Next is the Chapel of St Catherine, adorned with semi-precious stones. This is where Charles IV spent time in meditation – his portrait, with the second of his four wives, Anna von Schwednitz, is above the doorway.

Chapel of the Holy Cross

Finest of all, though, is the recently restored Chapel of the Holy Cross. It is divided into two sections by a golden railing; the precious relics were preserved in the sanctuary, which only the emperor and the priests were allowed to enter. The gold walls and ceilings of the chapel are studded with over 2,000 semi-precious stones (note also the 32 Venetian-glass stars embedded in the ceiling). The walls also feature 129 painted panels executed by Master Theodoric in the 1360s. More relics are set in the picture frames.

Zbraslav

Also to the south of Prague is Zbraslav ❷, just 12km (7 miles) along the River Vltava. It was once popular with day-trippers from Prague who swarmed off the paddle steamers (see www. paroplavba.cz for the modern equivalent) that had brought them to this rural spot to be entertained by the brass bands (of the Bohemian oom-pa variety) playing in pubs and riverside cafés. One of the most prolific Czech composers of waltzes and polkas for brass bands came from Zbraslav – a man named Jaromir Vejvoda. His catchy tune, 'Škoda lásky' ('What a Shame about Love') was one of the great hits of the mid-20th century, though it is better known abroad by its English or German titles ('Roll out the Barrel' or 'Rosamunde'). A restaurant on the town square is almost a shrine to Vejvoda and his music. Nowadays, however, most visitors come here for the National Gallery's Collection of Asian Art (tel: 257 921 638; www.ngprague.cz; Tue–Sun 10am–6pm; charge), housed in the 18th-century château.

DIRECTORY

A user-friendly alphabetical listing of practical information, plus hand-picked hotels and restaurants listings, clearly organised by area and to suit all budgets and tastes; a selection of entertainment venues is also given here.

A

AGE RESTRICTIONS

The age of consent for heterosexual, gay and lesbian sex is 15 in the Czech Republic. To buy and drink alchohol you must be 18 years old or over; the same restrictions apply for driving a car.

B

BUDGETING

In the past the Czech Republic has been a fairly cheap destination, but the koruna has strengthened against the pound, dollar and euro, making prices – at least for repeat visitors – feel relatively high. Expect to pay between £70–150 ($130–275) per night for a double room in a decent hotel. Eating out has risen in cost in recent years, but beer is still cheap, at around Kč60–70 a glass. A taxi into town from the airport will cost between Kč500–1,000, but it is perfectly possible to use public transport (bus then tram or metro to your destination): a basic transferable ticket costs Kč26 and a 24-hour ticket costs Kč100.

C

CHILDREN

Prague is generally a child-friendly destination, with a number of attractions either aimed at children or that both adults and children will find interesting. Children are usually eligible for reduced rates or even free entry for museums and galleries. Children up to 15 years old have reduced rates on public transport, and on certain tickets and days can travel for free if they are accompanied by a fare-paying adult.

CLOTHING

Prague has a mild version of the standard Central European climate of cold winters and warm summers. So normally you should take with you plenty of warm clothes, including gloves and a hat, for the winter, and light clothes for the summer. However, the weather can be changeable, so it is advisable always to have a light jumper or coat with you in the summer, and to carry an umbrella year round. If you intend visiting churches, then to avoid giving offence, you should be modestly dressed with covered shoulders and no shorts or short skirts.

CRIME AND SAFETY

Prague is a safe, pleasant city to explore on foot. Violent crime is rare, although petty crime such as car theft and pick-pocketing, especially on tram 22 or on Charles Bridge and in Wenceslas Square, has risen sharply in parallel with the growing number of visitors.

CUSTOMS

There is no restriction on the amount of foreign currency you can import and export. You must be able to prove, if

asked, that you have access to Kč1,000 per day or Kč37,000 per month with which to support yourself. In practice, you are unlikely to be asked. There is an import and export limit of Kč200,000. Keep your currency-exchange receipts as you may be required to show them. Travellers are allowed to import the following duty-free goods: 200 cigarettes or 100 cigarillos or 50 cigars or 250g of tobacco; 1 litre of spirits; 2 litres of wine; 50ml of perfume or 250ml of eau de Cologne. You can also import gifts up to a value of Kč6,000, as well as all reasonable items for personal use. It is illegal to export antiques without a permit.

D

DISABLED TRAVELLERS

Prague's public transport was not designed with disabled people in mind. Most metro stations and all trams and buses involve climbing and descending what can be very steep steps. People in wheelchairs who wish to use public transport must be carried bodily on and off trams and buses, and pavement kerbs do not often have ramps. But in general Praguers take a courteous view towards people with disabilities, and will make efforts to assist them.

E

ELECTRICITY

Electricity in the Czech Republic is at AC 220 volts. Two-pin plugs or adaptors are needed for UK appliances with three-pin plugs.

EMBASSIES AND CONSULATES

Australia: Klimentská 10, Prague 1; tel: 296 578 350.
Canada: Muchova 6, Prague 6; tel: 272 101 800; www.canada.cz.
Ireland: Tržiště 13, Prague 1; tel: 257 530 061.
New Zealand: Dykova 19, Prague 1; tel: 222 514 672.
South Africa: Ruská 65, Prague 10; tel: 267 311 114.
UK: Thunovská 14, Prague 1; tel: 257 402 111; www.britain.cz.
US: Tržiště 15, Prague 1; tel: 257 022 000; www.usembassy.cz.

EMERGENCIES

General emergency: tel: 112
Ambulance: tel: 155
Fire brigade: tel: 150
Police: tel: 158
Emergency road service: tel: 1230/ 1240
Lost or stolen credit cards:
American Express, tel: 222 800 222
Visa, Mastercard, tel: 272 771 111
Diner's Club, tel: 267 197 450

ETIQUETTE

Generally the Czechs are easygoing and very hospitable. However, they are not terribly impressed with the hordes of stag and hen parties that descend on their capital and cause mayhem. The

Above from far left: St Vitus's Cathedral; guard at the castle.

British in particular have a bad reputation for getting drunk and into trouble, even if the vast majority of visitors are – reasonably – sober and well behaved. When visiting a place of worship dress respectfully and do not expose too much flesh.

F

FESTIVALS

January
Prague Winter Festival
A commercial venture building on the success of the spring and autumn festivals, though not generally up to the standards of the other two. www.praguewinterfestival.com

January–February
12 Days of European Film
A festival split between the cities of Prague and Brno with diverse offerings from the European film industry. www.euro filmfest.cz

March
Opera – Musical Theatre Festival
A city-wide festival of musical theatre, including performances from youth theatres.www.divadlo.cz/jhd

March–April
Febio Fest
The largest international film festival in Central Europe. www.febiofest.cz

April
One World
A film festival of documentaries that focus on human rights. www.oneworld.cz

May
Four Days
An international festival of experimental theatre, as well as dance and music. www.ctyridny.cz

May–June
Khamoro
An annual festival of Roma culture with music and seminars. www.khamoro.cz

Prague Spring
This fabulous international music festival includes concerts at the Rudolfinum, Obecní dům and St Vitus's Cathedral. www.festival.cz

World Festival of Puppet Art
An enormous programme of live puppetry from around the world. www.puppetart.com

June
Prague Writers' Festival
This meeting of the minds draws some of the top scribes in the world. Past events were hosted by the authors Nadine Gordimer, Salman Rushdie and Gore Vidal. www.pwf.pragonet.cz

Prague Fringe Festival
A cultural exchange on a massive scale, in which performing artists from dozens of countries meet in Prague to render everything from puppetry to classical theatre and musical cabaret. www.praguefringe.com

Tanec Praha
A wonderfully diverse celebration of modern dance. www.tanecpha.cz

September–October
Prague Autumn
A young international music festival, not yet on a par with Prague Spring, but with some impressive visiting performers. www.pragueautumn.cz

November–May
Agharta Prague Jazz Festival
A bit of a misnomer, since this 'festival' is actually a series of high-quality concerts, usually one per month, from autumn to spring. Concerts are usually held at Lucerna Music Bar. Performers in recent years have included the Pat Metheny Group and saxophonist Joshua Redman. www. agharta.cz

FURTHER READING

Non-Fiction
Cities of the Imagination – Prague
Richard Burton (Signal Books 2003). A 'cultural and literary history' that gets beneath the skin of the city. Burton's discussions of key figures and events – from Jan Hus, alchemy and the Golem to Kafka, Hašek and the Velvet Revolution – are both insightful and thought-provoking.
Franz Kafka: a Biography Max Brod (Da Capo Press 1995). A reprint of the classic account of Kafka's life by his lifelong friend and editor.
Magic Prague Angelo Maria Ripellino (Picador 1994). More deftly than any other writer, Ripellino conjures up the esoteric ambience of the city in which strangeness was the norm, from the days of Rabbi Löw and Emperor Rudolf onwards.
We the People Timothy Garton Ash (Penguin 1990). Eyewitness account of the thrilling events of late 1989. British journalist and academic Garton Ash was present in the smoke-filled Laterna Magika theatre as students and dissidents prepared the peaceful overthrow of Communism.

Fiction
The Good Soldier Švejk and His Fortunes in the World War Jaroslav Hašek, translated by Cecil Parrott (Penguin 1973). While some prefer the pre-war, anonymous translation into English of the adventures of Hašek's iconic antihero (one of Penguin's very first publications), this version by a former British ambassador is 100 percent complete, omitting none of the beery conscript's many expletives and less-than-savoury exploits.
The Golem Gustav Meyrink (Dover Publications 1986). Written in 1913, this version of the legend of Rabbi Löw's clay homunculus is the classic version of the occult tale.
Prague Tales Jan Neruda (various editions). Charming short stories from the backstreets of the 19th-century city by the 'Dickens of Malá Strana'.
The Trial Franz Kafka, translated by W. and E. Muir (Penguin 2004). Also in Penguin Modern Classics and translated by the Muirs are ***The Castle*** and ***Description of a Struggle and Other Short Stories***. Kafka's creation of

shadowy worlds in which individuals are helpless in the face of an unfathomable authority was eerily prophetic of the atmosphere of Prague when it was in the grip of the totalitarian rule of Nazis, then of Communists. Despite the enthusiasm of today's tourist industry for his image, the contemporary city seems to have little left of the sinister character so tellingly evoked in his novels and short stories.

G

GAY AND LESBIAN ISSUES

Prague is generally very safe – though not necessarily out and proud – for gays and lesbians, and most people will encounter few problems. An excellent site for up-to-date information can be found at www.prague.gayguide.net. The main lesbian site (in Czech) is www.lesba.cz.

GREEN ISSUES

Large parts of the Czech Republic suffered from poor pollution control from Communist-era heavy industry, air pollution overall, however, has decreased by 50 percent since the 1980s, but there is still a long way to go. Stricter controls imposed by conditions of entry into the EU are already starting to have an effect.

Being situated between hills means air can become trapped in Prague, making winter smog more likely; a report by the Organisation for Economic Cooperation and Development

(OECD) revealed that the amount of nitrogen oxide in Prague is well above the EU and OECD average; a rapid increase in traffic levels in Prague since the 1989 revolution has exacerbated the pollution problem.

Carbon-Offsetting

Air travel produces a huge amount of carbon dioxide and is a significant contributor to global warming. If you would like to offset the damage caused to the environment by your flight, a number of organisations can do this for you, using online 'carbon calculators', which tell you how much you need to donate. In the UK travellers can visit www.climatecare.org or www.carbon neutral.com; in the US log on to www.climatefriendly.com or www.sustainabletravelinternational.org.

H

HEALTH

Visiting the Czech Republic poses no major health concerns and you do not need any inoculations. Citizens of EU countries, including the UK are entitled to free emergency treatment. Make sure you have your European Health Insurance Card before travelling. You will be charged for any further treatment, so it still makes sense to take out adequate health and accident insurance.

A number of medical facilities with English-speaking medical personnel cater specifically to visitors. For minor health problems Prague has modern

Above from far left: heading down into the metro; war memorial.

pharmacies (look for a green cross, or the word *lékárna* on the front of the shop), including 24-hour facilities at Štefánikova 6 and Palackého 5.

The Diplomatic Health Centre for foreigners (Na Homolce) is located at Roentgenova 2, Prague 5; tel: 257 272 146. For first aid visit Health Center Prague at Vodičkova 28, Prague 2; tel: 224 220 040.

HOURS AND HOLIDAYS

Most grocery shops are open weekdays 7am–6pm, with other shops open 10am–6pm, although those in the centre catering to the tourist trade often remain open late year-round. Smaller shops may close their doors for a couple of hours during lunchtime.

On Saturdays most shops outside the centre close at noon or 1pm, but shops in the centre, especially the large department stores, may retain weekday hours on Saturday and Sunday as well. The main commercial streets of Prague with dependably long hours year-round are Wenceslas Square and Na příkopě.

Public Holidays

1 January: New Year's Day
Easter Monday: variable according to the Roman calendar
1 May: May Day
8 May: Day of Liberation from Fascism
5 July: Feast Day of SS Cyril and Methodius
6 July: Anniversary of Jan Hus's death
28 October: Day of the origin of the independent Czechoslovakia
17 November: Day of Students' Struggle for Democracy, commemorating the Velvet Revolution
25–26 December: Christmas

I

INTERNET FACILITIES

These are widely available in Prague through many internet cafés in Malá Strana and the Old Town. It is likely that your hotel will have internet facilities and possibly also wi-fi in your room.

L

LANGUAGE

The national language is Czech. However, English is widely spoken, as is German. If you can learn a few Czech words, it will always be appreciated.

Pronunciation

Vowels: long vowels are indicated by an accent: á, é, í, ó, ú or ů and ý.
Ě like 'ye' in 'yes'
Ý long 'e' as in 'feet'
Au like 'ow' in 'now'
Ou like 'ow' in 'show'
L and r can be pronounced as half-vowels as in Plzeň (almost like Pulzen) and krk (almost like kirk).
Consonants:
C ts as in 'its'
Č like 'ch' in 'church'
Ch like 'ch' in 'loch'
J like 'y' in yes
R trilled or rolled
Ř (unique to Czech, and even diffi-

cult for some natives) a combination of
a trilled r and sh, as in Dvořák
Š 'sh'
Ž like 's' in pleasure

Basic Vocabulary

Good morning *Dobrý den*
Good evening *Dobrý večer*
Good night *Dobrou noc*
Hello *Ahoj*
Goodbye *Na shledanou*
Yes/No *Ano/Ne*
Please/you're welcome *Prosím*
Thank you *Děkuji*
Excuse me *Promiňte*
I'm sorry *Je mi líto*
Cheers! (when drinking) *Na zdraví!*
Help! *Pomoc!*
I am looking for… *Hledám…*
What? *Co?*
Where? *Kde?*
Where is/are? *Kde je/jsou?*
When? *Kdy?*
How? *Jak?*
How much? *Kolik?*
How much does it cost? *Kolik to stojí?*
I want *Chci*
We want *Chceme*
I would like *Chtěl bych* (*chtěla bych if
the speaker is female*)
I don't know *Nevím*
I don't understand *Nerozumím*
Do you speak English/German?
Mluvíte anglicky/německy?
Slowly, please! *Pomalu, prosím!*
Here *Tady*
There *Tam*

Numbers

0 *Nula*
1 *Jeden, jedna* (feminine), *jedno* (neuter)
2 *Dva, dvě* (feminine, neuter)
3 *Tři*
4 *Čtyři*
5 *Pét*
6 *Šest*
7 *Sedm*
8 *Osm*
9 *Devět*
10 *Deset*
A pair/few *Pár*
Half *Půl*

Days of the Week

Monday *pondělí*
Tuesday *úterý*
Wednesday *středa*
Thursday *čvrtek*
Friday *pátek*
Saturday *sobota*
Sunday *neděle*

LOST PROPERTY

To see if your lost property has been
handed in, tel: 224 235 085.

MAPS

Free maps are available from Around
Prague, the Prague Information Service.

MEDIA

Television and Radio
Satellite television has one or more
English-speaking news channels. The
main ones are CNN and BBC 24. Foreign broadcasts on Czech television are
dubbed rather than subtitled, although

there may be English-speaking programmes on other foreign-service television stations.

Radio Praha broadcasts news in English three times each day on 101.1 FM; www.radio.cz.

Press

All the main foreign-language newspapers are available at news-stands in the city. There are also several English publications printed locally and aimed at visitors to the city. *The Prague Post* (www.praguepost.com), published weekly, contains news and comment as well as events listings. A good resource is *Prague in Your Pocket*, a bimonthly publication highlighting various cultural events around the city. It also includes information on shopping, hotels and cultural festivals.

MONEY

The currency of the Czech Republic is the crown or koruna (Kč). Each crown is made up of 100 hellers (hal.). There are 5,000Kč, 2,000Kč, 1,000Kč, 500Kč, 200Kč, 100Kč, 50Kč and 20Kč notes; and coins of 50Kč, 20Kč, 10Kč, 5Kč, 2Kč, 1Kč and 50 hellers.

Exchange

There are many banks and bureaux de change in the city. Banks open 8am–4pm, but many close at lunchtime. Most charge a standard 1 percent commission. Bureaux de change have much more flexible hours, often open until 10pm, but can charge up to 30 percent commission, so it pays to shop

around. Hotels also change currency but their commission rates vary.

If you want to exchange remaining crowns back to your own currency before you leave the Czech Republic, you must have an official receipt for your original currency exchange.

Credit Cards, ATMs and Travellers' Cheques

Credit cards are increasingly accepted for payment across the city. They are now accepted by most hotels, but it is still wise to double-check before paying in a restaurant or a shop.

There are a large number of cashpoints that will issue cash against your current-account card or credit card; this is generally the easiest way to get money. Travellers' cheques offer a safe way of carrying cash and can be exchanged at banks, but stick to the major issuers. Note that they will not be accepted as payment in shops, restaurants or hotels.

Tipping

Tipping is appreciated, but levels are low, and in some restaurants service is included in the price – it should state this on the menu.

POLICE

State police are responsible for day-to-day policing. They wear white shirts and dark-grey trousers or skirts. They are armed. Municipal police wear light-grey trousers or skirts. Traffic

Above from far left: detail on the door of the Goethe Institute *(see p.70);* Ándel station.

police are responsible for all road and traffic regulations.

POST

Postal services are cheap and reliable for letters and postcards. Most shops that sell postcards also sell stamps, as do many hotels. Postboxes are either orange with a side slit or orange-and-blue with a front flap. The main post office (open 24 hours a day) is at Jindřišská 14, off Wenceslas Square. Here you can send telegrams, make international calls, and buy stamps and phonecards. Rates for sending letters and postcards change regularly.

R

RELIGION

Generally speaking the Czechs are suspicious of organised religion (only 19 percent of the population professes to believe in God) and the country is a secular republic. However, the dominant religion historically and with the largest number of believers is Catholicism.

There are many Jewish visitors to Prague, who come in search of its impressive Jewish heritage. For more information see www.kehilaprag.cz.

S

SMOKING

The only place free from tobacco smoke seems to be public transport; otherwise, the Czechs light up everywhere.

T

TELEPHONES

The international code for the Czech Republic is 420. The city code for Prague is 2, but this is included in the nine-digit number so should not be dialled in addition. Most phone numbers consist of nine digits, including the area code. Dial the entire nine-digit number even if you are dialling within the same area code. If you have problems getting through to a number, call Prague directory enquiries on 1180. Public telephones take phonecards *(telefonní karta)*. These can be bought at post offices or news-stands.

Mobile Phones

Most people will find that their own mobile phone will work in Prague (even if the charges will be much higher than using phonecards). However, for longer stays it is better and much cheaper to buy one of the easily available local pay-as-you-go SIM cards. The main companies are O2 (www.cz.o2.com) and Vodafone (www.vodafone.cz).

TIME ZONES

Prague operates on Central European Time (CET). This is one hour ahead of GMT in winter and two hours ahead of GMT in summer.

TOILETS

There are public toilets at each metro station, which should stay open until

Welcome to Prague

9pm. There is usually a small fee of around 2–5Kč.

If there are no man or woman symbols to help you, ladies' toilets will be labelled *Ženy* or *Dámy*, mens' will be *Muži* or *Páni*.

TOURIST INFORMATION

The Prague Information Service (PIS; Staroměstské náměstí; tel: 12 444; www.pis.cz) can provide much useful information, including city maps and and addresses. As well as at the main address above branches can be found at: Na příkopě 20; the Main Station; and in the Malostranská mostecká vez in Malá Strana.

TRANSPORT

Prague Airport

Prague's expanded and modernised Ruzyně airport lies about 20km (13 miles) northwest of the city. For flight information tel: 220 113 314 or check www.csl.cz. It is possible to book a flight to Prague from most European capitals and from New York, Montreal and Toronto. The flight from London takes about two hours. The national airline is ČSA (České Aeroline; www.csa.cz).

Numerous budget airlines now fly to Prague. From the UK these include: easyJet (www.easyjet.com), flying from Gatwick, Bristol, East Midlands, Newcastle and Stansted; BMIbaby (www.bmibaby.com) from Birmingham, Cardiff, East Midlands and Manchester; and Jet2 (www.jet2.com)

from Belfast, Edinburgh, Leeds-Bradford and Manchester. The Czech-based Smart Wings (www.smartwings.net) flies Barcelona, Budapest, Dubai, Heraklion, Las Palmas, Madrid, Paris, Rome and Valencia.

From North America the only airline to fly direct to Prague, from New York and Toronto, is ČSA (www.csa.cz). For visitors coming from other starting points in Canada or the US, it might would more sense to fly direct to London and then connect with a flight on one of the carriers listed above.

Transport from the Airport

The cheapest way into the city from the airport (or vice versa) is by city transport. There are public bus services to the metro at Dejvická (buses 119 and 254), probably the most useful for the majority of visitors, the metro at Zličín (bus 100), and the metro at Nové Butovice (buses 179 and 225). The journey by bus 119 or 179 takes about 30–45 minutes (15 minutes by bus 100) and tickets are available from either the DPP counter in the arrivals hall or from machines by the bus stop just outside the terminal building. If you arrive late at night a night bus (510) will take you to the tram stop at Divoká Šárka, where you can pick up the night tram (51) into town.

A private minibus shuttle service, Čedaz (tel: 220 114 296; www.cedaz.cz), operates between the airport and náměstí Republiky with a stop at Dejvická metro station, every half-hour between 5.30am and 9.30pm. The journey between the airport and the

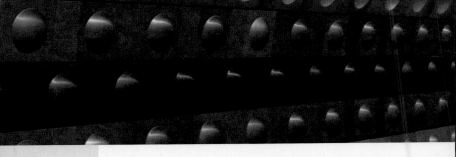

náměstí Republiky terminus takes 30–45 minutes. They also have a number of minibuses that will take you directly to your hotel for a fee. However, the rates are almost as high as by taxi.

Two taxi firms operate from the airport into town, Airport Cars and AAA (tel: 140 14). Both have desks at arrivals. Taxis are lined up outside the arrivals exit. Rates are relatively high, however; a ride to the centre will cost around 650Kč.

By Train

The most direct way to reach Prague from London by train is via Paris and Frankfurt, which takes around 18 hours (for details and booking check with www.raileurope.co.uk). Some of these trains arrive at Smíchov.

Public Transport

Prague has a comprehensive and integrated public-transport system that provides a cheap and efficient service. The extremely efficient Prague metro opened in 1974 and provides a great service for visitors. There are three interlinked lines, and metro maps can be found at each station. Metro signs above ground feature a stylised M incorporated into an arrow pointing downwards. Metro trains operate until midnight.

Buses tend to provide a service out to the Prague suburbs rather than compete with trams in the city.

Tickets and passes can be used on all forms of transport. Each ticket has a time limit, and you pay more for a longer limit. The cheapest ticket costs Kč18 and allows either 20–30 minutes of travel with no transfer or five stops on the metro with no line change. A Kč26 ticket allows 75 minutes of travel and allows line change or tram transfer within that time. Children aged six to 15 pay half-price.

Tickets can be bought at metro stations (there are automatic ticket machines which give instructions in English and supply change) or newsstands. They must be validated in the small yellow machines you will see when you catch the tram or arrive at the metro.

Day tickets or longer passes are also available and are valid for unlimited travel on all forms of transport. These can often be supplied by your hotel concierge but can also be purchased at the m.h.d. kiosks at all major metro stations. They will be valid from the date stamped on them and do not have to be validated for each journey. Prices are as follows: 24-hour pass Kč100; three-day pass Kč330; and five-day pass Kč500.

There is a comprehensive network of 31 tram routes, which connects both sides of the river. Each tram stop shows the tram number passing there and a timetable. Most city maps show the tram routes in addition to the location of the major attractions. All trams run from 4.30am–midnight, but a number of routes are also designated as night routes and operate a service 24 hours per day. Purchase your ticket before you travel and validate it as you enter unless you are transferring from another tram or metro within your allotted time.

Taxis

There are some unscrupulous operators, and overcharging is a common complaint. Phoning a taxi is cheaper than hailing one, as rates are lower and you won't be overcharged. Two reputable firms with staff who speak English are AAA Taxi (tel: 140 14) and Profi Taxi (tel: 844 700 800). If you must hail a taxi, check the rates listed on the passenger door with the meter, or negotiate a price beforehand; a ride in the city centre should not cost more than Kč100–200, a trip to the airport about Kč650.

Driving

Even for drivers who know Prague, the city can be a traffic nightmare. Large sections of Staré Město and Malá Strana have been completely closed to traffic. If you do manage to get through the maze of one-way streets and culs-de-sac to find yourself in the centre you'll probably be turned away by the police (or may even get a ticket) unless you can prove you are resident at one of the hotels nearby. It is therefore highly advisable to leave your car at home and explore the city either on foot or by public transport.

V

VISAS AND PASSPORTS

Citizens of the European Union (EU) – of which the Czech Republic is now a member – and of most European countries need only a passport to visit the Czech Republic for up to 180 days.

Citizens of the US, Canada, New Zealand and Australia can stay for up to 90 days with a passport. Citizens of South Africa can enter the Czech Republic but must first obtain a visa. All passports must be valid for at least three months from the date of your arrival in the Czech Republic.

W

WEBSITES

There are websites given in the text throughout the book, but, in addition to those, here are a few of the main ones: www.czechtourism.com (the main Czech tourism authority); www.dpp.cz/en (Prague public transport); www.pis.cz (the Prague Information Service); www.praguepost.cz (the *Prague Post* newspaper).

WEIGHTS AND MEASURES

The Czech Republic uses the metric system of measurement.

WOMEN

Although feminism still has a long way to go in the Czech Republic, women travelling in Prague and the Czech Republic should not expect to encounter any particular problems. If you are by yourself late at night, however, the usual rules of common sense apply. Keep in mind that pubs in Prague can be very male-dominated environments, and solo women may not feel comfortable in them.

Hradčany (Castle District)

Hotel Hoffmeister

Pod bruskou 7; tel: 251 017 111;
www.hoffmeister.cz; metro: Malostranská; €€€€

On the corner of Chotkova as it winds up past the castle, the Hoffmeister is in a very convenient location. Not as attractive as some Prague hotels from the outside, but with rooms and facilities that are luxurious. Comfortable and tasteful, and with an excellent spa – for which it is well known – and restaurant. The prices are surprisingly good compared to some other Prague five-stars.

U krále karla

Nerudova/Úvoz 4; tel: 257 533 594;
www.romantichotels.cz; tram: 22,
23; €€–€€€

This Baroque building (it took its present form in 1639) is in a quiet and convenient location at the top of the hill, looking out over Petřín Hill and the Strahov. The rooms lean a little more towards Central European kitsch than some, but many people will love the stained-glass windows.

U raka

Černínská 10; tel: 220 511 100;
www.romantikhotel-uraka.cz; tram:
22, 23; €€€

Set in one of the only wooden houses left in Prague, and dating back to the mid-18th century, this complex is now a lovely hotel. The spotless rooms are beautifully laid out, and there is a delightful garden for the use of guests.

One of the more expensive places to stay, but quiet and romantic.

Malá Strana

Dům u tří čápů

Tomášská 16; tel: 257 210 779;
www.utricapu.cz; tram: 12, 22; €€€

This newly opened design hotel close to the Waldstein Palace is excellent. Very chic, all clean lines and modern furniture, but without disturbing the original fabric of this historic building. The rooms are not only beautifully done but very central and quiet, and the café and restaurant good places to while away a few hours.

Dům u velké boty

Vlašská 30; tel: 257 532 088;
www.dumuvelkeboty.cz; tram: 12,
22; €–€€

Opposite the German Embassy, this small hotel is in a superb location. The building dates from the early 17th century, and care has been taken to ensure that the interior and furniture maintain the historic feel. Lovely comfy beds, spotless bathrooms and friendly owners all go towards making this one of the best places to stay in the city. They accept cash only.

Hotel Aria

Tržiště 9; tel: 225 334 111;
www.ariahotel.net; tram: 12, 22;
€€€€

Expensive but heavy on designer chic, this newish addition to Malá Strana plays heavily on its musical theme. From Mozart to Dizzy Gillespie, each floor and room is dedicated to a par-

ticular music or musician. The fittings and fixtures are classy, as is the in-house music library.

Hotel Neruda

Nerudova 44; tel: 257 535 557; www.hotelneruda-praha.cz; tram: 12, 22; €€€

A stone's throw away from the castle, this building dating from 1348 now has a minimalist modern interior. You are paying for the location as much as anything, but the rooms are clean and comfortable, and there is a pleasant café space where you can sit and sip hot chocolate.

Mandarin Oriental

Nebovidská 1; tel: 233 088 888; www.mandarinoriental.com; tram: 12, 22; €€€€

Cleverly inserted into the fabric of a 14th-century monastery in the tranquil heart of Malá Strana, this luxury establishment offers superlative comfort in a historic setting. As well as individually designed bedrooms and stylish public spaces, there is a spa offering a sophisticated range of treatments.

Residence Nosticova

Nosticova 1; tel: 257 312 513; www.nosticova.com; tram: 12, 22; €€€

If you have the money, this could be a delightful place to stay. Set above the excellent Alchymist restaurant, the fairytale apartments are beautifully furnished (one even has a grand piano), and all have an attached bathroom and kitchen. There are large reductions for stays during low season.

Staré Město

Four Seasons Hotel

Veleslavínova 2a; tel: 221 427 000; www.fourseasons.com; metro: Staroměstská; €€€€

As well as an unsurpassable location close to Charles Bridge and with views over the Vltava to Malá Strana and the castle, the Four Seasons offers all the comfort and style associated with its name. A bonus is its Allegro restaurant, up there with Prague's finest.

Hotel černý slon

Týnská 1; tel: 222 321 521; www.hotelcernyslon.cz; metro: náměstí Republiky; €–€€

A lovely 14th-century building on the the Unesco protected list, very close to Old Town Square. The simple but attractive rooms – those in the attic are particularly nice with their wooden beams – are excellent value, and the price includes breakfast.

Hotel Josef

Rybná 20; tel: 221 700 111; www.hoteljosef.com; metro: náměstí Republiky; €€€–€€€€

A sleek designer hotel near the Jewish Quarter. The interior, designed by Eva Jiřičná, has stone-and-glass bathrooms attached to minimalist rooms with

---

Price for a double room for one night without breakfast:

€€€€	over 250 euros
€€€	180–250 euros
€€	120–180 euros
€	below 120 euros

DVD and CD players. None of this is cheap (up to around 350 euros per night), but it does make a change from the often heritage-heavy accommodation available elsewhere in the city.

Hotel Paríz

Obecního domu 1; tel: 222 195 195; www.hotel-pariz.cz; metro: náměstí Republiky; €€€€

More luxury in this squeaky-clean Art Nouveau building from 1904. Unfortunately the rooms have been rather over-restored and the original furniture replaced with bland modern pieces that make a nod towards the original style. The Restaurant Sarah Bernhardt has fared rather better and retains its sparkling interior and wooden fittings.

Nové Město

987 Prague

Senovázné náměstí 15; tel: 255 737 200; www.987hotels.com; metro: náměstí Republiky; €€€€

In the north of the New Town is this über chic design hotel. Newly opened with Phillip Starck fixtures and Aera Saarinena and Arne Jacobsen furniture, it epitomises a certain kind of northern European cool design. Great if you like it, but this is not the

> Price for a double room for one night without breakfast:
>
> €€€€ over 250 euros
> €€€ 180–250 euros
> €€ 120–180 euros
> € below 120 euros

cheapest place in town. They are due to open a more funky take on the same theme, the 987 Soho, at Na Porící 42 during 2009.

Carlo IV

Senovázné náměstí 13; tel: 224 593 111; www.boscolohotels.it; metro: náměstí Republiky; €€€€

A very grand 19th-century building painstakingly converted into a luxury hotel. The interior designers have let their imaginations run riot with sumptuous rooms, a chic restaurant and a fabulous spa and swimming pool. It can also be fabulously expensive, but perhaps worth it for this very continental version of stylish comfort.

Hotel Elite

Ostrovní 32; tel: 224 932 250; www.hotelelite.cz; metro: Národní třida; €

Not many hotels in the New Town have a suite protected by the municipality, but the Elite has, due to a 17th-century painted ceiling. The other rooms have also been tastefully preserved, with wooden floors, period furniture and an uncluttered feel. There is a pleasant courtyard bar and café for the summer, and the Ultramarin restaurant.

Hotel Palace

Panská 12; tel: 224 093 111; www.palacehotel.cz; metro: Můstek; €€€

A Secessionist landmark, built in 1909 as a luxury hotel. It still performs this function today, though now it is only the façade that retains its Art Nouveau appearance. The

interior was gutted in the 1980s to make way for comfortable, if a little impersonal, modern rooms. However, this act of vandalism is offset by the luxury and excellent service.

Hotel Yasmin

Politických vězňů 12; tel: 234 100 100; www.hotel-yasmin.cz; metro: Muzeum; €€€

Just one block away from Wenceslas Square, this newly opened hotel has a more playful approach than some of the more po-faced designer hotels elsewhere in the city. Graced by loud contemporary artworks and with comfortable rooms (check out the sumptuous bathrooms), this is a winner. The chic noodle bar is not a bad place to eat either.

Penzion u svatého Jana

Vyšehradská 28; tel: 224 911 789; www.usvjana.cz; metro: Karlovo náměstí; €

Right next door to the Church of St John on the Rock, this newish hotel is set in the church's neo-Baroque administrative annexe. The large rooms are fairly bare but clean, and the building is grand and in a quiet location.

Further Afield

Andel's

Stroupežnického 21, Prague 5; tel: 296 889 688; www.andelshotel.com; metro: Anděl; €–€€

Although this glass-and-steel hotel may seem a little corporate at first, it has nice designer touches, elegant rooms and a luxurious feel. This all comes at surprisingly good price (due as much anything to the location, but it is still only 10 minutes away from the centre by metro).

Hotel Adalbert

Břevnovský klášter, Markétská 1, Břevnov; tel: 220 406 170; www.hoteladalbert.cz; tram: 22, 36; €–€€

This hotel is in an excellent and beautifully quiet location inside the Břevnov Monastery; convenient for both the city centre (by tram) and airport (by bus). The 18th-century building is very attractive and the comfortable rooms are excellent value.

Hotel Praha

Sušická 20, Dejvice; tel: 224 343 305; www.htlpraha.cz; tram: 2, 8, 36; €€€€

Out towards the airport, this 1980s Stalinist undulating concrete ziggurat has managed to turn its previous incarnation as a place exclusively for apparatchiks to its advantage; there is a certain chic to its Modernist bulk, large rooms and built-in security measures. Aside from these, there are garden terraces and excellent service.

Pension Vyšehrad

Krokova 6, Vyšehrad; tel: 241 408 455; www.pension-vysehrad.cz; metro: Vyšehrad; €

A quiet, friendly, family-run pension with impressive views and a very attractive garden. There are only four simple but comfortable rooms, and a small dining room with a patio.

Above from far left: plump pillows and reception at the stylish Hotel Josef; Wellness Centre at the Hotel Paríz.

Hradčany (Castle District)

U Císařů

Loretánská 5; tel: 220 518 484; daily 11am–midnight; €€€

This restaurant's name translates as 'At the Emperor's', and, appropriately, is just on the other side of the square from the Castle. The old-fashioned Czech menu includes wild boar, pheasant and duck, though there are, surprisingly, also a few vegetarian dishes.

Malá Strana

Alchymist

Tržiště 19; tel: 257 286 019; www. alchymisthotel.com; daily noon–3pm, 7pm–11pm; €€€€

Decorated in upmarket bordello style, this restaurant is the place to come if you have done rather well out of the post-Communist privatisations. If you can afford to ignore the prices, the food and long wine list are of a good standard.

Kampa Park

Na Kampě 8b; tel: 296 826 102; daily 11.30am–1am; €€€

The food is good, and the views over the river are spectacular. The steep prices, however, may cause some indigestion. Popular with local celebrities.

Price guide for a two-course meal for one with a glass of house wine:

€€€€	over 60 euros
€€€	40–60 euros
€€	20–40 euros
€	below 20 euros

Pálffy Palác

Valdštejnská 14; tel: 257 530 522; daily 11am–11pm; €€€–€€€€

Go through the door in the right-hand side of the imposing gateway and up the stairs to reach a dining hall that epitomises faded glory: all gilded chandeliers and yellowing walls. The food, a combination of French and Czech, is competent but unremarkable, but it is the surroundings that really count.

U Modré kachničky

Nebovidská 6; tel: 257 320 308; daily noon–4pm, 6.30pm–midnight; €€€

This charming Bohemian restaurant serves fine duck and game dishes. Try venison with bilberries and spinach or duck with walnut stuffing. Make sure you save space for the lovely fruit dumplings for dessert.

U Patrona

Dražického náměstí 4; tel: 257 530 725; daily 10am–midnight; €€€€

These elegant little dining rooms close to the Charles Bridge are a good place to try some well-prepared Bohemian specialities. Dishes include game consommé with juniper berries and roast goose with red cabbage.

Staré Město

Allegro

Four Seasons Hotel, Veleslavínova 2; tel: 221 427 000; daily 7am–11pm; €€€€

Often hailed as the best restaurant in the city, Allegro was the first recipient of a Michelin star in post-Communist Eastern Europe. Breakfast, lunch

and dinner are served either in the dining room, or, in the summer, on the outdoor terrace with its views across the river to the castle. Menus offer a delicious array well-thought-out dishes, many with an Italian twist courtesy of chef Vito Mollica.

Ariana

Rámová 6; tel: 222 323 438; daily 11am–11pm; €–€€

Strange as it may sound, this Afghan restaurant in an old Prague building proves an excellent formula. The Persian-inspired dishes comprise kebabs, curried vegetables and specialities such as steamed bread stuffed with vegetables. Big mounds of rice accompany most dishes. Wash it all down with a yoghurt drink or sweet chai.

Arzenal Siam-i-Sam

Valentinská 11; tel: 224 814 099; daily 10am–midnight; €€

Furniture, glass and ceramics are sold at the front of Arzenal-Siam-i-Sam, the brainchild of Czech designer Bořek Šípek, while at the back is an excellent Thai restaurant with good service and a stylish interior. The spicy, authentic dishes are beautifully presented – the idea is that you can also buy the dishes and glasses out front. The large menu includes many vegetarian options.

Bellevue

Smetanovo nábřeží 18; tel: 222 221 443; daily noon–3pm, 5.30–11pm; €€€–€€€€

Smart restaurant serving a competent version of modern international cuisine.

Some dishes can be over-elaborate, such as venison carpaccio and mushroom-tomato concassé flavoured with truffle oil, cognac and port wine reduction seasoned with sarawak pepper.

Brasileiro

U Radnice 8; tel: 224 234 474; daily 11am–midnight; €€

One of the successful Ambiente group of restaurants, the Brasileiro specialises in Uruguayan and Brazilian beef offered on an 'as-much-as-you-can-eat' formula. Wash your meal down with wine from Uruguay.

Café Montmartre

Retězová 7; tel: 222 221 244; Mon–Fri 9am–11pm, Sat–Sun noon–11pm; €

Historic café, once frequented by writers such as Jaroslav Hašek and Egon Erwin Kisch. Though no longer a hotbed of political and cultural debate, it remains a pleasant place to sit, read and drink.

Café Slavia

Národní třída/Smetanovo nábřeži; tel: 224 218 493; daily 8am–11pm; €

This famous café, with its views over the river and National Theatre, was once the haunt of artists and writers, including Václav Havel. The spacious and elegant Art Deco interior encourages you to linger, and morning coffee turns into lunch with a range of salads, pancakes and Czech dishes.

Dahab

Dlouhá 33; tel: 224 827 375; daily noon–1am; €–€€

Above from far left: fashionable restaurant; back-to-basics dining.

Watch the Bill
Diners need to keep a watchful eye on the bill in Prague. Menu prices include value-added tax, but some waiters persist in adding it again to the total. In some of the more expensive restaurants, beware of trays of *hors d'oeuvres* you may be offered; far from being complimentary, they may add substantially to the bill. Other items such as bread, butter, olives and mayonnaise also often cost extra.

An Arab coffee house recreated in central Prague, complete with narghiles, mint tea and couscous. There is a large selection of teas, excellent Turkish coffee and a varied menu of Middle Eastern food, including good vegetarian dishes.

Don Giovanni

Karolíny světlé 34; tel: 222 222 062; daily 11am–midnight; €€€
A long-established Italian restaurant serving surprisingly authentic dishes. There is also a good range of Italian wines, including one from the owner's vineyard, and some excellent *grappa*.

Ebel Coffee House

Týn 2; tel: 224 895 788; daily 9am–10pm; €
This café situated in a courtyard behind the Týn Church offers some of the best coffee in Prague. Their roasts can be bought, along with a variety of teas, at their nearby shop Vzpomínky na Afriku (on Rybná/Jakubská). The café also serves a selection of light meals.

Flambée

Betlem Palais, Husova 5; tel: 224 248 512; daily noon–midnight; €€€€
An expensive but high-quality French restaurant that runs a close second to Allegro *(see p.116)* as the city's best restaurant. The rich but beautifully cooked food makes full use of luxury ingredients such as foie gras and truffles.

Káva Káva Káva

Národni třída 37; tel: 224 228 862; Mon–Fri 7am–10pm, Sat–Sun 9am–10pm; €

A pleasant, quiet café in a courtyard opposite Tesco. The friendly staff serve excellent coffee in vast mugs as well as a selection of bagels, quiches and cakes. There is also internet access downstairs.

Obecní dům

Náměstí republiky 5; tel: 222 002 770; Francouzscá restaurace: Mon–Sat noon–4pm, 6–11pm, Sun 11.30am–3pm, 6–11pm; Plzeňská restaurace: daily 11.30am–11pm; Kavárna Obecní dům: daily 7.30am–11pm; €–€€€
Prague's most opulent Art Nouveau building is home to three eateries. The finest, Francouzscá restaurace, is a pricey French restaurant offering passable food within a spectacular gilded and chandeliered interior. On the other side of the lobby is the café Kavárna Obecní dům, which serves more basic meals and cakes amid equally impressive surroundings. Downstairs in the basement is the cheaper, smartly decorated, Plzeňská restaurace, serving tasty Czech dishes.

Orange Moon

Rámová 5; tel: 222 325 119; daily 11.30am–11.30pm; €€
This Thai, Burmese and Indian restaurant is housed in a simple tiled cellar. Dishes range from chicken satay and spring rolls to phad thai and fish masala. The food is hot, spicy and tasty.

Pizzeria Rugantino

Dušní 4; tel: 224 815 192; Mon–Sat 11am–11pm, Sun noon–11pm; €€
Handily close to Old Town Square, this restaurant serves large, tasty pizzas at

reasonable prices. There is a no-smoking section at the front, overlooking the street, and the staff are friendly.

U medvídků

Na perštýně 7; tel: 224 211 916; Mon–Sat 11.30am–11pm, Sun 11.30am–11pm; €€

This traditional beer hall, founded in 1466, is friendly, bustling and noisy. Excellent Budvar beer washes down a succession of classic Czech dishes, including garlic soup, pork with cabbage and dumplings and the ubiquitous fried cheese.

Josefov

Barock

Pařížská 24; tel: 222 329 221; Mon–Fri 10am–1am, Sat 10am–2am, Sun 10am–1am; €€€

Like its partner Pravda, this is a place for posing rather than gourmet food. Espressos and calorie-laden breakfasts are replaced by international dishes at lunch, before the space turns into more of a bar later in the evening. Large pictures of minimally dressed models provide the decor.

Potrefená husa

Bílkova 5; tel: 222 326 626; daily 11am–midnight; €€

Situated in the basement of one of Prague's Cubist buildings, the 'Shot Goose' appeals to the younger generation of diners with a well-designed interior, moderate prices, updated Czech dishes and a good choice of drinks. It is one of a successful chain, with other branches around the city.

Nové Město

Albio

Truhlářská 20; tel: 222 325 414; Mon–Sat 11am–10pm; €–€€

This excellent vegetarian restaurant serves tasty and inventive dishes, many cooked with organic ingredients. The menu (printed on recycled cardboard) gives lots of nutritional information, and the dishes range from salad with grilled goat's cheese and walnut oil to tasty noodle dishes. The ginger beer is definitely worth a try, as are the unpasteurised Bernard dark and light ales. The same owners run a well-stocked organic supermarket next door.

Alcron

Radisson SAS Alcron Hotel, Štěpánská 40; tel: 222 820 038; Mon–Sat 5.30–11pm; €€€

Dating from the 1930s, the Radisson Hotel offers wonderful period decor as well as this decent fish restaurant. A varied menu, ranging from South-East Asian to French dishes, uses fresh ingredients.

Café and Galerie Louvre

Národní třída 20; tel: 224 930 949; daily 8am–11.30pm; €

An elegant Art Nouveau café, much loved in the past by Prague's intellectuals, Café and Galerie Louvre is a great place to sit and browse through the papers. Below the café proper is a café-gallery displaying contemporary art, while upstairs you can get good-value breakfasts and light meals throughout the day.

Vinárna

Traditionally, a *vinárna* was an establishment serving wine rather than beer, often from a particular region or even vineyard. Nowadays it is simply another term for a restaurant with some pretensions to refinement.

Café Imperial

Na poříčí 15; tel: 246 011 440; daily
7am–11pm; €€

One of the grand old cafés of Prague,
the Café Imperial is worth a visit just
for the restored Art Nouveau interior
with its wonderful tiling. Breakfast,
lunch, afternoon tea and evening meals
are served by friendly staff.

Celnice

V celnice 4; tel: 224 212 240; daily
11am–midnight; €€

Another Pilsner Urquell-owned beer
hall, with all the advantages they bring
of excellent beer and calorific Bohemian
food. Celnice has the advantage of being
on top of one of Prague's best clubs,
where you can dance off the dumplings.

Cicala

Zitna 43; tel: 222 210 375; Mon–Sat
11.30am–10.30pm; €€

Set in a basement off a busy street,
Cicala serves the most authentic, and
some of the tastiest, Italian food in the
city. The menu offers antipasti, pasta
and meat dishes, plus daily specials.

Globe Bookstore
and Coffeehouse

Pštrossova 6; tel: 224 934 203; daily
9.30am–midnight; €–€€

Well known as a centre of ex-pat intellectual life. As well as the friendly café,
with good coffee and light meals
(pasta, salads and burgers), the book
shop has occasional live music, lectures
and book readings and signings. It is
also one of the most pleasant, and
cheapest, places to check your email.

Pivovarský dům

Ječná/Lípová 15; tel: 296 216 666;
daily 11am–11.30pm; €€

This microbrewery and restaurant is
noted for its wide and varied range of
beers brewed on the premises (even
including coffee and banana beer). The
hearty Czech food (such as roast pork
and stuffed dumplings) is tasty and
helps to soak up the drink. Among the
other offerings are a wheat beer, mead
and a delicious dark beer.

Universal

V Jirchářích 6; tel: 224 934 416;
Mon–Sat 11.30am–12.30am,
Sun 11am–midnight; €€

A well-priced, comfortable French
bistro serving good food. Once settled
in the slick interior, you can choose from
dishes such as *salade Niçoise*, steaks, and
some classic desserts. Recommended.

U Fleků

Křemencova 11; tel: 224 934 019;
daily 9am–11pm; €€

An ancient and well-known brewery
with an illustrious past. Its present is
not so admirable, filled as it is with
hordes of tourists who bash tables,
scoff down the goulash and quaff beer.
However, the dark beer, brewed on site,
is just as wonderful as ever. Avoid the
'free' Becherovka.

U Pinkasů

Jungmannova 16; tel: 221 1111
150; daily 11.30am–1am; €€

While the ground floor and basement
of this traditional establishment are
given over to rather serious drinkers

of Plzeňský prazdroj (on tap here since 1843), the more genteel upper floor is an attractive restaurant serving a range of authentic Bohemian dishes.

Vinohrady and Žižkov

Pizzeria Grosseto

Francouzská 2/náměstí Míru; tel: 224 252 778; daily 11.30am–11pm; €–€€

Popular with local residents and office workers, this friendly restaurant serves some of the best pizza in Prague (all freshly cooked in a wood-burning oven). If you enjoy this one you might want to look out for their branches in Dejvice (Jugoslávských partyzánů 8) and Průhonice (Květnové náměstí 11).

Radost FX

Bělehradská 120; tel: 224 254 776; Mon–Sat 11am–1am, Sun 10.30am–midnight; €

Connected to the popular club of the same name, this vegetarian restaurant offers a wide range of dishes inspired by cuisines from the Mediterranean to Mexico to China.

Restaurant Atelier

Na Kovárně 8; tel: 271 721 866; Mon–Sat noon–midnight; €€–€€€

Smart French restaurant situated just to the east of Havlickovy sady. The cooking is of a high standard, free from gimmicks and offered at very reasonable prices. As well as a summer terrace, there is an impressive list of French wines.

Restaurant Myslivna

Jagellonská 21; tel: 222 723 252; daily 11am–11pm; €€

Not far from the landmark Television Tower, this restaurant specialising in game is intended for the dedicated carnivore. If it is furry and lives in the Bohemian forest, there is a very good chance you can eat it here. The wild boar and venison are recommended.

Taverna Olympos

Kubelíkova 9; tel: 222 722 239; Mon–Sat 11.30am–midnight, Sun 11.30am–11pm; €

Cheerful and extremely popular Greek establishment, with a garden section that is popular with families. Greek wine as well as the usual range of tasty Hellenic comestibles.

U vystřeleného oka

U božich bojovníků 3; tel: 222 540 465; Mon–Sat 4.30pm–1am; €

Despite plenty of competition, the 'Shot-Out Eye' is still one of the best pubs in Žižkov. Excellent beer is served up in bizarre and louche surroundings, all authentically smoky and generally with loud music playing.

Holešovice

Hanavský Pavilon

Letenské sady 6; tel: 233 323 641; daily 11am–1am; €€–€€€

The pavilion, an eccentric neo-Baroque building dating from the 1891 Exhibition, is perched on the edge of the Letná Park escarpment, with spectacular views over the city. The traditional Czech menu comprises trout, pikeperch, duck, pigeon and game dishes, as well as a good selection of Moravian wines.

Above from far left: Globe Café Bookstore; upscale restaurant.

Children
Prague restaurants are gradually becoming more attuned to the needs of visitors with young children, and some restaurants now have non-smoking sections, provide high-chairs and offer children's menus. Child-friendly establishments include Pizzeria Rugantino, Pizzeria Grosseto and others, such as Taverna Olympos, with seating outside.

There is something for everyone in Prague, from top-flight classical concerts, to jazz, cinemas and clubs. One of the city's charms is that whatever you are into, you will find the venues relaxed and not as concerned with appearances as might be the case elsewhere.

To purchase tickets it is best to go directly to the box office in order to get the lowest price (and for many places you can book tickets directly on-line). However, if you do need to go to a ticket agency, try one of the following:

Bohemia Ticket
Malé náměstí 13; tel: 224 227 832; www.bohemiaticket.cz

Ticket Art
Politických vězňů 9; tel: 222 897 333; www.ticket-art.cz

Ticketpro
Pasáž Lucerna, Štěpánská 61; tel: 296 329 999; www.ticketpro.cz

Ticketstream
Koubkova 8; tel. 224 263 049; www.ticketstream.cz

Classical Music, Theatre and Ballet

Národní divadlo (National Theatre)
Národní třída 2; tel: 224 901 448; www.narodni-divadlo.cz

Opera, ballet and theatre performed by the National Theatre ensembles. This is also the location of the **Laterna magika** 'Black Light' theatre *(see p.21)*.

Obecní dům (Municipal House)
Náměstí Republiky 5; tel: 222 002 336; www.obecnidum.cz

The splendid Art Nouveau Municipal House has one of the best concert halls in the city and is home to the Prague Symphony Orchestra (www.fok.cz).

The Rudolfinum
Alšovo nábřeží 12/náměstí Jana Palacha; tel: 227 059 227

This is the home of the Czech Philharmonic (www.ceskafilharmonie.cz) and the Prague Radio Symphony Orchestra (www2.rozhlas.cz/socr). The main concert season runs from October to May.

Státní Opera Praha (Prague State Opera)
Wilsonova 4; tel: 224 227 266; www.opera.cz

Productions here are usually of a very high standard. The repertory provides a mix of 19th-century opera and more daring contemporary works.

Stavovské divadlo (Estates Theatre)
Ovocný trh 6; tel: 224 901 448; www.narodni-divadlo.cz

Opera, dance and theatre; *Don Giovanni* was premièred here in 1787, conducted by Mozart himself. His operas are still regularly staged here. Part of the National Theatre network.

Jazz Clubs

Agharta jazz centrum
Železná 16; tel: 222 211 275; www.agharta.cz

Since its move to more spacious accommodation in the autumn of 2004 this has become a more comfortable, if more formal, venue. This is a good

place to catch top local musicians. and it organises an ongoing jazz festival, attracting classy foreign bands.

Charles Bridge Jazz Club

Saská 3; tel: 257 220 820;
www.jazzblues.cz

A new, small club in Malá Strana that has a good list of local talent. Music starts at about 9pm and booking a table is advised. Unusually for a Prague club it is non-smoking.

Jazz lounge U staré paní

Michalská 9; tel: 603 551 680;
www.jazzlounge.cz

A home for jazz fans, this 100-seat club draws in some of the best musicians from the Czech Republic and abroad.

U Malého Glena

Karmelitská 23; tel: 257 531 717;
www.malyglen.cz

Intimate (read tiny) basement that is home to some of the finest jazz in Prague. Good acoustics and a decent bar add to the attractions.

Ungelt Jazz & Blues Club

Týn 2; tel: 224 895 748

A youngish club with lots of funk and blues, aimed more at visitors than locals, with a cosy stone interior and a casual, informal crowd. The programme can be seen at www.prague.tv.

Cinemas

English-language films in Prague are usually shown with Czech subtitles. The following places have more daring selections of new and classic movies:

Kino Aero (Biskupcova 31; tel: 271 771 349; www.kinoaero.cz); Evald (Národní třída 28; tel: 221 105 225; www.cinemart.cz); and MAT Studio (Karlovo náměstí 19; tel: 224 915 765; www.mat.cz).

Nightlife

Club Celnice

V celnice 4; tel: 224 212 240;
www.clubcelnice.com

Underneath the New Town restaurant and bar of the same name, this is currently one of Prague's best places for a night out. Very popular, with a well-dressed crowd.

Mecca

U průhonu 3; tel: 283 870 522;
www.mecca.cz

Large and flash, the Mecca attracts top local DJs and packs club-goers in for its party nights. Jazz nights courtesy of Jazz Club Železná.

Radost FX

Bělehradská 120; tel: 603 181 500;
www.radostfx.cz

Still the king of dance clubs, with a good crowd and top local and international DJs playing lots of house and R'n'B. The restaurant is one of the best vegetarian places in town.

Roxy

Dlouhá 33; tel: 224 826 296;
www.roxy.cz

One of the best spaces in town, with an eclectic mix of top foreign DJs and contemporary art shows. There are also screenings of experimental cinema.

Above from far left: National Theatre auditorium; interior of the Estates Theatre.

CREDITS

Insight Step by Step Prague
Written by: Alfred Horn, Maria Lord and Michael Macaroon
Series Editor: Clare Peel
Cartography Editors: Zoë Goodwin, James Macdonald and Neal Jordan-Caws
Picture Manager: Steven Lawrence
Production: Kenneth Chan
Photography: AA World Travel Library/ Top-Foto 6-2, 82; Agharta Jazz Centrum 21-1; Aria Hotel 112; Pete Bennett /APA 7-2, 11-3, 24-5, 30-3, 38-1,2, 55-2, 87-2, 88; Dům u velké boty 113; Galerie Rudolfinum 20-1; Glyn Genin/APA 2-7, 4-3,5, 8-6, 10-1, 15-1, 18-1,3, 24-1, 27-2,4, 30-1, 40-1, 46-2,3,4, 47, 53-2, 54-4, 63-1,2, 65-1, 68-1, 69-1,2, 70-1, 75-2, 79-2, 80-2, 81-1, 89-2, 92-2,4; Hemis/Alamy 84/85; Hotel Joseph 98-6, 114-1,2; Hotel Pariz 115-1, 121; iStockphoto.com 8-4,7, 12-1, 13-2,3, 14-2, 17-2, 26-1, 48-1, 49-1,2, 50, 51, 64-1,2, 77-1, 117, 119-1; Maria Lord 2-4, 6-1, 26-2, 29-1, 60-2, 89-1, 98-1,4, 102/103, 110/111, 116; Michael Macaroon 2-5,6, 6-3,4, 8-5, 10-4, 12-2, 17-1, 18-2, 27-1, 30-2, 33-1, 36-1, 37-1, 40-2,3,4,5, 42-2,3, 43-2,3, 44-2, 48-2, 52-2, 54-1,2, 59-1, 61-1, 62-1, 64-3,4, 65-2, 67(all), 68-2, 90/91(all), 92-3, 98-2, 118-2; Museum of Decorative Arts 61-2; Narodni Divadl 98-5, 122, 123; Profimedia International s.r.o./Alamy 94-1; Rod Purcell/APA 2-1,2,3, 4-1,2,4, 6-5, 7-1,3,4,5, 8-1,2,3, 10-2,5, 11-1,2, 12-3,4, 13-1, 14-1,3,4,5, 16, 18-4, 19(all), 21-2, 24-2,3,4,7, 27-3, 28-1,2, 29-2, 31-1, 33-2,3, 34-1,2, 35(all), 36-2, 39-1,2, 41-1, 43-1, 44-1, 45-1,2, 46-1, 52-1, 53-1, 54-3, 55-1, 56/57(all), 58, 59-2, 60-1, 62-2, 70-2, 72(all), 73(all), 74(all), 75-1,2, 76-1, 77-2,3, 78-1,2, 79-1,3, 80-1, 86-1,2, 87-1,3, 92-1, 93-1,2, 95, 96, 97, 98-3,7, 100, 101, 104, 105, 106, 107, 108, 109, 118-1, 120; Mark Read/APA 22, 42-1; State Opera Prague 20-2, 66-1,2; Phil Wood/APA 10-3, 23, 24-6, 29-3,4, 31-2,3, 32, 38-3,4, 71-1; World Pictures/Photoshot 83.

Cover: main image: Simeone Giovanni/SIME-4Corners Images; front left: Nordicphoto/Alamy; front right: Bill Wassman/APA

Printed by: Insight Print Services (Pte) Ltd, 38 Joo Koon Road, Singapore 628990

© 2009 APA Publications GmbH & Co. Verlag KG (Singapore branch)

CONTACTING THE EDITORS

We would appreciate it if readers would alert us to errors or outdated information by writing to us at insight@apaguide.co.uk or APA Publications, PO Box 7910, London SE1 1WE, UK.

www.insightguides.com

DISTRIBUTION

Worldwide
APA Publications GmbH & Co. Verlag KG
(Singapore branch), 38 Joo Koon Road,
Singapore 628990
Tel: (65) 6865 1600
Fax: (65) 6861 6438

UK and Ireland
GeoCenter International Ltd
Meridian House, Churchill Way West,
Basingstoke, Hampshire, RG21 6YR
Tel: (44) 01256 817 987
Fax: (44) 01256 817 988

United States
Langenscheidt Publishers, Inc.
36–36 33rd Street, 4th Floor,
Long Island City, NY 11106
Tel: (1) 718 784 0055
Fax: (1) 718 784 0640

Australia
Universal Publishers
1 Waterloo Road, Macquarie Park,
NSW 2113
Tel: (61) 2 9857 3700
Fax: (61) 2 9888 9074

New Zealand
Hema Maps New Zealand Ltd (HNZ)
Unit 2, 10 Cryers Road
East Tamaki, Auckland 2013
New Zealand
Tel: (64) 9 273 6459
Fax: (64) 9 273 6479

INDEX